IN THE
HEART
of a Child

In The
Heart
of a Child

A. Lynn Scoresby

Bookcraft

SALT LAKE CITY, UTAH

Library of Congress Catalog Card Number: 87–70403
ISBN 0–88494–626–6

First Printing, 1987

Printed in the United States of America

To the children in my heart:
Daniel, Stephanie, Brendan, Jeremy,
Brett, Jon, Jennifer, and Ashley

Contents

1   In Our Children's Hearts

This book discusses Latter-day Saint parenthood in the context of covenants meant to bind families together for eternity. It is not an attempt to prescribe specific rules and methods of raising children. It is not meant to make parents feel responsible for everything, good or bad, that their children do. It is, rather, a presentation of ideas I have discovered, tested, used, and refined during my years as a father, teacher, psychologist, and Church worker. These are ideas that I have found to make family life more enjoyable for both parents and children. Like all the ideas I have ever found truly useful, these ideas are firmly rooted in the gospel of Jesus Christ.

I have talked with and taught many young people. Some of these young people are already intelligent, moral, and committed to high ideals. Others of them have fallen into self-destructive attitudes, beliefs, and behaviors that have brought them and their parents pain, which only those who know it from experience will ever understand.

As a branch president at the Provo Missionary Training Center, I have contact with young people who should be among the finest of LDS youth. As I have interviewed missionaries from many parts of our country and from many other countries, I have found that some missionaries indeed come to the work already devoted to God and committed to performing any required task. They recognize sacred things and find great joy in doing anything they believe to be in service of others. There are other missionaries, however, who are not ready for the work. These people find rules frustrating, and they make jokes when sacred subjects are being discussed. Some of these missionaries are crude in their conversation, and they offend the

Spirit of the Lord by their pranks and their foolishness. Like other less mature and less constructive people, these missionaries require help and support from others so that they can learn a better way to live.

It is natural for us to wonder what makes the difference between these two kinds of young people. It is helpful in coming to an answer to give close attention to the specific behavior of individuals in the two groups. Missionaries who are already prepared and committed think about themselves differently from those less committed. They talk of testimony, love, concern for others, sacrifice, and dedication. These words reflect an inner understanding of gospel ideals, as opposed to a focus on external conditions in the world around them. Their conversation reveals an awareness of true ideas, and their behavior shows that they know how to apply these ideas in their lives. They go about their work quietly, and usually they do it well, completing assigned tasks, often without supervision. They usually keep the same standards when they are alone as when around other people.

Those less prepared for missionary work speak more often about superficial things, about things external to them. They seem most concerned about impressing others, and to do this they may give exaggerated accounts of personal achievements. They usually perform best when they will be noticed, and often they do not work at all when no one is around to watch them. Their values and behavior change according to circumstance; they tend to adopt the attitudes, mannerisms, and actions of the people they are with.

It is tempting for us as parents and teachers to spend a great deal of energy worrying about what is wrong with the young people who cannot seem to do what we think they should do. These children disturb us with their actions and force us to pay attention to them because of their misbehavior. I believe it is helpful for us to resist this temptation and focus instead on what it could be that enables some young people to discover the good that is in them, to form values consistent with the teachings of Jesus Christ, and to live according to those values. For the most part, young people who are not yet able to do this are just immature. As they gain experience, they will acquire the wisdom that will improve their behavior. In the meantime, however, some will be unproductive, some will be immoral, some will find the sights, sounds, tastes, and other sensations of the world so alluring that they are unable to perceive anything else as worthwhile. We fear they will never break out of this, will never mature. As a matter of fact, some may not. This is justifiably disturbing, sad, and painful to us.

But if we spend all our time thinking about the problems these children present, we may never come to ponder how the other ones, the ones with mature conviction of right and wrong, come to be as they are. For parents who wish their children to live righteously, there is little more important.

Let us consider, then, what it is that helps children develop an inner and deeper understanding of the gospel and the capacity to live according to that understanding. Is there something we can do to ensure this process? Or are we left just hoping that our children will be among the lucky ones who "turn out all right"? I believe that we *can* give our children some important help in this regard. In order to do this, however, we must first understand something about ourselves as parents and about our children, and then be willing to apply certain basic skills that help children believe in and live by what they are taught.

How to Know a Child's Heart

To begin with, as parents we can think of our children much as our Heavenly Father thinks of us. He is most interested in our development and growth toward immortality and eternal life. We should be most interested in our children's development from infants toward successful, mature adults. Having passed through mortality before us, God understands what this experience is like for us; He knows, and He teaches what will be most helpful to us. Like Him, we have lived longer than our children. We have once been children and can remember our childhood experiences. Good or bad, our early experiences influence what we teach our children. As our Heavenly Father has with us, we have a lasting relationship with our children and will be forever influenced by what they become even as they are influenced by what we teach them. This thought alone ought to motivate us to know thoroughly about ourselves and our children so that we can help them focus their attention on developing spiritual commitment and on expressing it through their many personal attributes.

After knowing many children, some very well, I am convinced that to fully understand them we must know how children develop. For most of us this knowledge comes after we have reared our children and we say to ourselves, "Now that I am through raising children, I finally have learned how to do it." But we can learn about child development before and while we are rearing our children, we can know them better, and we can know what helps them along the way. This book provides information about child development and integrates these ideas with the principles of the gospel.

Likewise, the skills we use to teach our children this inner understanding and dedication to the gospel need not come only by the trial and error of experience. There are some gospel principles which, if applied by us in our relationships with our children, will promote spiritual maturity. Many of these principles are described in this book and can be integrated with ideas about child development to help parents to improve their skills. By getting a little better at what we do, we can more fully ensure that our children will be given every opportunity to grow toward an understanding of and devotion to the truth.

One of the most exciting parts of parenthood comes when we experience firsthand that each child has built-in promises of personality that we can watch unfold and perhaps influence. As our lives become intertwined with our children's we share one experience after another, which shapes both them and us. Having lived a few years more than our children, we are usually able to see both the excitement of what is to come and the possible pitfalls which might hurt them. Parenthood often means sitting on this sharp edge where we wish for good experiences for our children but do not want them to be hurt by what they choose or by what happens to them. In all of it, we appreciate even more the wonder that is a developing child. Even though we may not always be able to speak our feelings, still we know and are assured that we are participants in the greatest enterprise life will offer.

Child development is such a complex process that behavioral scientists, after seventy-five years of studying it, still have not been able to describe everything about it. Fortunately, we do not have to know everything about what happens between birth and adulthood in order to help children grow in the gospel. But it helps if we have a basic perspective on the entirety of childhood. When we have some idea about what happens to children during the first eighteen to twenty years of life, we can understand at any moment what children might need from us to help them along the way. When we do not have this perspective we are more likely to get caught in the "moment," living from crisis to crisis, conflict to conflict. After years of this we may view our children with regret, observing that they have become something other than what we want them to be. What we have taught them is not what we wanted them to learn, and now it is too late to have them develop what might have been a real commitment to what is true. The more we know about the way children develop, the more likely we are to be able to help them find experiences to prepare them for a mature spiritual life.

A serious student of child development can study in many areas: physical maturation, intellectual development, social and emotional growth, language acquisition, moral aspects of the human personality. Each of these areas, and others like them, have been the object of much research and writing. There is a great deal to learn if we want to study for ourselves. Most of us, however, will be able to read little more than a small amount of what is available. But this will be sufficient. We must remember that our objective is not to learn everything about child development, but to gain an overall perspective. Gaining this perspective begins, I think, with the idea that growth and development are always taking place as long as there is life. It is wise for us frequently to remind ourselves that this growth has a direction and leads to some conclusions. Our influence, our children's inherited abilities, and their experiences combine to promote their development toward potentials that exist from birth, even if we cannot see the actual results until after children have grown into them. There is abundant evidence that what children inherit directs them toward very specific personality traits, interests, styles of judgment, and physical appearance. Constance Golden wrote about identical twins who were reunited after years of separation because of adoption ("Twins Reunited," *Science Magazine*, 1985). She described the research of Thomas Bouchard, who has found instances where twins, even though they were not reared in the same circumstances, showed amazing similarities as adults. Two of the brothers studied were thirty-nine years old when they met for the first time. Both had law enforcement training and worked part time as deputy sheriffs. Both vacationed in Florida, both drove

Chevrolets. Both had dogs named Toy. One had a son named James Allan, the other a son named James Alan.

It would seem that there are traits and interests our children are likely to develop if something does not prevent it. Latter-day Saints understand that the potential for godhood is born within each child, but that each child is also an individual with an eternal identity of his or her own. This concept, applied to child development, may be called understanding the "growth potential," which eventually becomes an "identity," the set of enduring personality traits that characterize each person for life.

One of my children showed early that he had an ability to be friendly to others, including strangers. He easily met new children and made them his friends, whether he was at home or away. Growing up, he had so many acquaintances in so many places that it was difficult for us to keep track of them. We didn't know when he was ten how this ability would later be demonstrated during his mission, in his career choices, and in his family relationships. This trait has become part of his personality and will probably endure for the rest of his life. But, looking back now, it seems obvious that we could have predicted this part of how he would be at age twenty-one and later.

Another idea that contributes to an overall perspective on children's growth can be called the *added upon principle*. This principle suggests the way identity develops. Anything children experience can be integrated into an identity, and repeated experiences are more likely to be "added" than isolated ones. If children experience repeated failures, for example, they will eventually learn helplessness and form a "failure" identity. If, on the other hand, children are repeatedly successful, they will be likely to form a "success" identity. This principle applies to traits, such as honesty or kindness, as well as to performance skills, as in athletics and music. Knowing that children add characteristics to their personalities in proportion to the frequency of the experiences that create the characteristics, we can influence and create experiences for our children that will help them develop according to our desires.

A third idea about child development that I believe is important to a proper perspective is called the *progression principle*. This principle recognizes that children's growth goes from simple things to more complex. In every area of development (e.g., physical, emotional, social, or mental) they start out learning basic skills such as crawling, then go to walking, then running. Each new development is more complex than the one preceding it. Most parents easily recognize this progression in their children, but we often do not appreciate that if we knew the order of their development we could know when to teach them certain things that we want them to know and teach in a way that will have the greatest effect. We are also able to tell that children do not develop according to their chronological age but according to a biological clock they inherit. This means we cannot rely on their age to tell us what and how to understand them. We must watch their actions, listen to their speech, and understand their emotions in order to tell what we must do to help them grow in their understanding of the gospel. Even the Savior, we are informed, did not receive a fulness at first, but grew grace on grace until he knew or received it all. (D&C 93.) This suggests, I believe, that to know the hearts of our children, we must pay sensitive attention to the periods of their progression. Some of these are described in subsequent chapters.

If we approach parenthood knowing about these "sensitive periods," then we will recognize that we must prepare to adapt somewhat to different children and to adapt as children grow older in order to match what we do with what our children need. Failure to do this can be very bad for our children. I have known several good teenage children who were struggling with parents attempting to regulate them with the same discipline used when the children were much younger. Some of these teenage children were intelligent and moral, but most were very unhappy. They could not progress because they were frustrated by their parents' failure to adapt. When these parents were able to adapt their discipline to better fit their children's levels of development, both parents and children were much happier, and the children progressed.

Even more, however, most children require that we have an intimate awareness of their emotional needs, desires, dreams, and talents. Then we communicate that we know them by the way we talk to them, discipline them, and encourage them to develop their talents; they form an abiding trust in our judgments and become more teachable. If we can remember that every child is motivated by emotional needs, we can help them feel love, a sense of belonging, and self-control. These three are basic to all children as they grow and mature.

The concept of growth potential suggests that children have urges and impulses to progress in their current direction. If they have repeated experiences with love, sacrifice, unselfishness, and other inner qualities, these will add upon one another until children's hearts are full of them. If children repeat anger, fear, selfishness, and other similar attributes, these will be added upon until a child's heart is full of these. The result of these feelings and experiences is to fear others, to seek to impress them, and to think little of inner truths. The progression principle suggests that periods of time exist in which children are more teachable and require that we adapt to them as they grow. Taking the time to nurture them, understand them, and adapt to them will help us lead them.

The Law in Children's Hearts

We may think of parenthood as work we do out of obligation to our children. We may think of it as our lifetime's greatest joy. Sometimes we might think that parenthood consists mostly of happiness and satisfaction; other times it seems to be worry, frustration, anger, despair, and sorrow. The experiences which create all these feelings can consume our thoughts and prevent us from remembering our most important task: teaching our children the importance of knowing the Lord. To the prophet Jeremiah, the Lord spoke of his own desire for his children to know him:

> This shall be the covenant that I will make with the house of Israel. . . . I will put my law in their inward parts, and write it in their hearts . . . for they shall all know me, from the least of them unto the greatest of them. (Jeremiah 31:33-34.)

This passage directs us to the Lord's emphasis on the inner place (heart) where his law (gospel) is to be written. This could mean in one sense that his teachings are to be understood through thoughts and feelings that become intentions and motives, and then, after being nurtured by the Holy Ghost, become faith, service, and dedication. The Lord says further that He will place his law in people's hearts because they know Him. All shall know Him, from the greatest to the least. I believe this means that knowing God and His Son is the primary means by which people are caused to reflect on their inner experience with the gospel. There are many gospel words which describe what is within us. Some of these are dedication, love, sacrifice, compassion, and charity. All of these are attributes of Jesus Christ. To truly know Him, I believe we and our children need to know and express these same attributes. Knowing the Savior well leads one to think about whether he is charitable, for example, instead of whether he is famous. When children actively try to develop these characteristics, they will receive a testimony from the Holy Ghost, who bears witness to their souls that Jesus is the Savior and Redeemer and that God is the Eternal Father. This knowledge and understanding—won through personal effort in daily practice and prayer—enables us to be sensitive to our own thoughts and feelings and to those of others.

When people are focused on that which is material, worldly, and external to themselves there is little interest in knowing the Lord. Diffusion and distractions are evident in their lives. Instead of striving to follow Christ, such people (1) are likely to pursue sensual excitement through drink, improper sex, stealing, and other thrills, (2) seek for positions of power, wealth, or status, or (3) live with no ambition other than eating, sleeping, and staying comfortable.

When we see that our first and most important task is to teach our children about the Savior and to know of His inner law of the gospel, we lead them to quieter paths, which some children might mistake as less exciting but which bring the creativeness, joy, peace, and calm that all who are wise yearn for. The reality of this beautiful kind of life came to me vividly as I talked to one Elder at the MTC. I asked him to tell me how he learned about the gospel. He was twenty-five years old, tall, handsome, and quiet. As we sat together silently, before he answered my request, tears welled in his eyes, spilled over, and ran down his face. He could speak only with difficulty. He told me had graduated from college. He had studied business and played on the university basketball team. He described how he found work in a large city nearby and was living by himself. He felt that he needed something else because of the type of life he was living and the loneliness he felt. He found it in the gospel; leaving his job and his friends, he wished most of all to serve the Lord on a mission. I wish everyone could have the privilege of watching such a young man conduct meetings, love the other missionaries,

and lead them with enthusiasm and spirituality. When it was time
for him to leave the MTC, he came and embraced me, and I embraced
him in return. We were brothers, loving the same Savior.

Covenants of the Heart

Children know the Savior by learning to be like Him; then they
learn about covenants, promises made between the Savior and them.
These are ordinances of the priesthood like the endowment and
sealing, in which power is given to unite hearts and souls. We have
been taught that the most important work we do is within our own
families, so that the children who are born into our care become our
most important responsibility in this world. Knowing this, believing
this, and committing ourselves to this gives us the focus we need to
do for our children what they need us to do. This is the best preparation we can make for parenthood, because the attention we give
to the covenants of our eternal family will be noticed and learned by
our children, who will in time participate in this covenant of the
heart. We have already helped our children a great deal by just
coming to this point of focus and commitment. Having a true conviction of our rule in God's plan for His children gives us a stability
that will help our children write the gospel in their hearts and form
their own enduring identities as sons or daughers of God.

If we are constant and stable, we will help our children be
strong individuals who, when facing quiet trials of temptation, will
choose the right. These children, unlike those who are "tossed about"
by one stimulus or another, will hear the still, small voice, and they
will have a vision of the part they play in an eternal plan, performing the service required of them by the Lord without having to be
pressured to do so. They will be missionaries who labor long and
hard without apparent reward or constant supervision. They will be
like Daniel, or Esther, or those prophets and Saints who dared honor
God at the risk of rejection by friends, persecution by enemies, or
even death.

When we are able to appreciate and honor the covenants we
have made with God and with our family, we are more likely to be
able to prepare our children to perpetuate their birthright as children of the covenant, and in so doing we perpetuate ourselves. This
does not mean that none of our children will ever make a mistake
or go astray, or that none will doubt or question or sin. It does not

mean that if a child falls to the wayside we are wholly to blame. It merely means that if we have the gospel written in our own hearts, it will be easier for us to help our children write it in theirs.

The Promise of Eternal Lives

Most parents understand to some degree the great beauty of the blessings that we are promised if we honor our covenants with God to multiply and replenish the earth and do his work among our fellowmen. Abraham was promised that in his descendants, all the nations of the earth would be blessed. This must have been a great satisfaction to Abraham, that from him would come so much joy to the world. For any righteous person, the knowledge that he can bless the lives of others is a great joy. But note that Abraham was not promised that all his descendants would be righteous. If we take too much hope, evaluating ourselves by our children, we could remember that Lucifer is a son of God, that all of us, bad and good, are God's children. And we don't hold God responsible for that. It is better for us to hope our children will be righteous, teach them with hope and commitment, and give them increased freedom as they grow, knowing they may use it unwisely. Through righteous children God establishes his covenants and fulfills his promise to bless all who will be blessed. And it is a very great reward indeed to be the instrument of such blessing.

I had an experience in May 1984 which made this vivid for me. I went with my wife, my brother and his wife, and my father on a family pilgrimage to northern England. My paternal grandfather had emigrated in the late 1880s from North Yorkshire. He was born in the town of Wetwang. He emigrated because of an opportunity to buy farm land. He wanted to be a farmer and an animal owner. He went with his brother, John, and together they homesteaded land near Ipswitch in Queensland, Australia. They had lived and worked there for three years when they received word that their family in England was in financial difficulty and wanted one of the sons to return. William, my grandfather, stayed and developed the land. Eventually he married a woman who was the daughter of other homesteaders. Her name was Jessie Higgs, and they settled on his homestead of about 160 acres and began their family.

A few years later, my grandmother's brothers met the LDS missionaries. Their first contact took place close to the turn of the twentieth century. They were quite interested by what they heard the missionaries say and invited my grandfather and grandmother to a meeting. After several months of study, all were baptized. This took place just before my father, the fourth child in the family, was born in 1903.

My father has told me what he knows of his father's character. He said that Grandfather smoked prior to hearing the gospel. After he learned that smoking was not a wise thing to do, he decided to quit—and did so that very day. He never smoked again, nor did he drink coffee or alcohol. He was also quite a spiritual man who, after learning the truth, was willing to make any sacrifice for his religion. One day as he was walking down the street of a little town near his farm, he heard a voice say, "Come out of Babylon." He and my grandmother had been trying to decide whether to stay in Australia or come to the United States. The statement he heard meant to him that he should do whatever was necessary to move closer to Zion.

I can appreciate the fact that a voice speaking to my grandfather would speak in scriptural language. Grandfather knew the scriptures well and loved them. (The Spirit wouldn't say, "Pack up and go to the States, Bill.") Having received a divine message, he sold his farm— virtually gave it away—and in 1906 moved his family to the United States. They first attempted to land in San Francisco, but found there had been a huge earthquake which prevented any landing. They had to sail northward to Vancouver, British Columbia, and from there they came by rail to a small town in southeastern Idaho.

Although they never saw their relatives in England again, my grandparents corresponded with them, and my father continues this to the present day. Though unseen, these relatives have been important to us. My father and mother sent food and clothing to them in England during World War II. We knew their names and occasionally saw a picture of them on a birthday or holiday. The real purpose of our visit to England in 1984 was to finally meet a first cousin, who was eighty-one—the same age as my father.

The years have been kind to my grandfather and his posterity. My father had four brothers and one sister. After settling in southeastern Idaho, they lived in poverty, but through sacrifice and work began to buy farmland and prosper. My father's younger brother was killed at age nineteen and so did not marry and have a family. My father has six children, one uncle had two children, one had ten children, one was the father of one son and one daughter, and my aunt had a son and a daughter. These grandchildren have all married and have children so that now there are 128 direct descendants of William Scoresby and Jesse Higgs. Sixty-four of my grandparents' descendants have served missions. Three returned to Australia, two have gone to England, and the others have been in various parts of the world.

As I stood in the little town of Wetwang, in beautiful North Yorkshire, I thought of my grandfather. He had heard the voice of God and had made a covenant to keep God's commandments. And like father Abraham, he had a posterity that blessed the lives of many people. My grandfather, who had joined the Church and lived a faithful life, had a posterity totalling 128 individuals in three generations. Those people who stayed in England didn't have the advantages we have had in the United States, nor have they accepted the gospel with its teachings about families. My grandfather's brother has only 9 descendants in comparison to my grandfather's 128. For me, this has become a living example of the promise of our covenant.

As Latter-day Saint parents, I believe it is important for us to teach our children that they are children of promise and that they are part of an eternal family, the family of God. In return for God's promise to call them His, they promise to honor their birthright by participating in God's work, including parenthood, if it comes to them. It is our greatest joy when our children capture the vision of themselves as sons and daughters of God and live to be like Him. We and they can go on in peace, humbly and courageously knowing that with God all can be overcome, all is possible. When they choose the right while young, avoid temptations to do evil as they mature, and make eternal priesthood covenants as they enter adulthood, then they will show that the law is truly written in their hearts.

2   Parent's Progress

We usually have to be parents for a while before we discover that we know more than we can actually do. By then we often feel we are too tired to do anything to improve. So, when someone suggests that we do something better, we nod wearily and agree, but our backs, feet, and head may ache so much that any attempt would be feeble. What we often don't realize is that getting better at parenthood might not require much change.

I believe it is possible for every parent to learn how to help children understand and live by the Savior's teachings. Instead of thinking it to be a huge, difficult task, most of us need only continue what we are doing now and perhaps make a few minor adjustments. There are, of course, a few parents who know, as do their children, that major changes are required for them. But for all of us it is helpful to recognize that our progress comes from making what we already do well into something even better. This requires some consistent effort, but it is not exhausting or impossible.

Sometimes we feel so much pressure to be good parents that we create stress for ourselves that makes us less capable of doing our best. Then, being less than we hope for or expect, we find decreased enjoyment and satisfaction. In contrast, those who do the best job of parenting are also those who enjoy it most. One task then is to learn how to enjoy many kinds of involvement—changing diapers, dressing or playing with or talking to children, putting them to bed. It is also important to relax and let ourselves enjoy what we already *do* enjoy. One mother wanted to know how long she should nurse her baby. "Do you enjoy nursing?" I asked. "Oh yes," she bubbled, "it is a great time to be alone with him." "Why not do it as long as you want, then?" I asked. "Well," she said, then paused as if her enjoyment was not sufficient reason, "will the baby be all right?" "It will if you are all right," I told her. "Babies do best when mothers are enjoying them."

As we think about what we can do to help children comprehend the gospel, one essential step is for us to comprehend parenthood. There are many ways we encourage success or contribute to failure. There are many ways to help children feel loved or condemn them to live in loneliness. We cannot control everything in our children's lives, so we have to decide how to balance freedom and regulations. But, whether we are often present or often absent, whether we earn our children's trust or fail them, we influence their lives.

Children are best helped to learn any idea from us, especially the truths of the gospel, when we are confident not only in the idea or principle but also in ourselves as parents. This means that we ought not to be afraid to learn new skills. This does not mean that when we encounter a new idea from reading or from listening to a speaker we immediately attempt to apply it haphazardly. A confident parent will think carefully about an idea before using it on the family. Too many of us have times of quiet desperation because we are insecure, and in our eagerness and caring we too quickly try any idea that seems good.

Contrary to what many teach, I believe that there is one best way to be a parent, especially when we are trying to help children learn to live the gospel. This method is to think about ourselves and what kind of parent we would like to be and then gradually progress until we have achieved those desires. This is comprehending parenthood—being wise enough to acquire knowledge and then fitting the knowledge to suit ourselves. We will not be able to help our children understand what we teach them if we are busy trying out others' ideas without making them our own. It goes without saying, of course, that the ideas presented in this book should therefore be adapted to suit *your* version of parenthood.

Making ideas our own means testing them against our own experience before we accept them. If something works for us (e.g., it helps our children progress), then we are likely to make it our own. In gospel terms, an idea about parenting succeeds if we and our children grow in the direction of our Heavenly Father as a result of what we do. Love works between parents and children, for example, because it is a characteristic of God. So does faith, sacrifice, unselfishness. Abuse and indifference do not help children because these are not God's characteristics. All that we think of doing as parents can be tested against these standards: Does it help our children progress? Do we find satisfaction in doing it? Are we helped by it to become more like our heavenly parents?

For many years we have read and listened to statements extolling the currently most popular approach to child rearing. This approach is based on a *child-centered* philosophy. This philosophy emphasizes knowledge about children and sensitivity to their emotional needs, as well as the obligation to protect children and nurture them. There is much that is positive about this philosophy because parents who follow it will be more caring and aware than neglectful and abusive. The quality of parenting has improved because of child-centered care.

There is, however, one negative by-product of child-centered parenting. The founders and supporters of this orientation were caught up in the need for parents to treat children in humane and nurturing ways because historically children have had a very rough time of it. They could not have foreseen, however, that parents can be overly concerned about children. Such excessive sensitivity to children's feelings has prevented some parents from doing or saying what they thought best, because of the fear that children's feelings might be hurt.

Many who embraced the ideals of sensitive and devoted care for children also believed that if children are good, successful, or talented, then parents have been good, successful parents. The opposite logically follows from this reasoning: if children fail, parents have failed, too. This creates the idea that one person's success can depend on someone else's actions. Because of this, some parents try to avoid the guilt associated with possible failure by anxiously doing everything, teaching everything, giving everything to be *super* parents. Others try to be *controlling*; they sometimes succeed, sometimes fail, and often feel great frustration. A few others make efforts to help children succeed, find it to be difficult and unpleasurable work at times, and gradually become *indifferent* in order to avoid the frustrations other parents live with. All these reactions to parenthood obviously reduce the fun of it. Children can be harmed by exaggerated behavior of all these types—super, controlling, or indifferent.

Many wonderful, committed people are parents of children who do not live as their parents would like them. Many wonderful, committed children come from families where parents were much less than competent. While there is a link between what we do and how our children turn out, we are not the whole cause of how they live, good or bad. All we can do is our very best, which involves knowing the difference between what we can do something about and what we cannot.

Learn to Enjoy Being a Parent

If we assume that enjoying parenthood will help our children and will help us be better parents, for our children's sakes we should find ways to increase the pleasure of it. One way to do this is to measure our success not only by what our children do but also by the way *we* act. This requires that we decide for ourselves what we most want to do and be as a parent. We may, for example, select being patient, communicating, loving, and touching as some of our criteria of success. Then we might experiment to find the exact ways we want to express these characteristics. Then all that is required is for us to progress until we become what we want. Though this usually takes a while, it is fairly easy along the way to keep thoughts about how we act as parents separate from wrong thoughts that we are the sole cause of how our children act. Eventually, we will feel less helpless, because we have the courage to be responsible and do our best at the same time as we see our efforts attempt to bring about good things in the lives of our children.

A second important way to increase the enjoyment of parenthood is to understand human progression. No one will be as good a parent at the beginning as he or she will be after gaining experience. Though we all know this, we seldom appreciate the need to be patient with our mistakes and with our children's. There are few, if any, parent or child actions that must be perfect. We only need to gradually get better little by little. One neighbor of mine recognized this concept when she told of her exasperation at trying to teach a daughter to be organized and keep a clean room. After years of struggling, arguing, and never really succeeding, the daughter married. Suddenly, motivated by a desire for her husband's approval, this slovenly daughter became fastidious. The mother's anger and frustration would have been lessened had she accepted earlier that children's abilities and parental standards sometimes happily coincide, but not often.

If we truly love our children and invest time and interest in parenthood, we will be good enough for what is needed. If our intentions are to improve, we need not heap pressure and guilt on ourselves when we are less than wonderful. Our children will not find a miserable life because of mistakes made in loving effort. They will more likely resist us if we err through indifference or if we attempt perfection and, failing, berate *them* because of *our* guilt at our failure.

A third way to enjoy parenthood more is to acquire a sense of personal responsibility. Simply put, this means that no program, no set of guidelines, no strategy of discipline will bring satisfaction to parents and success to children unless it is firmly rooted in personal values and beliefs. Parents must accept that they are the only ones who care enough to do what has to be done. None of us can fully rely on schools or church programs to do what we cannot. At best they assist us. And sometimes they do not help at all, or may even do harm. No one knows your children as you do. No one knows exactly what is important to you. If you take an idea and reflect on it to see how it feels to you and fits into your plan, then it will more likely work because you have made it your own. There is no best scientifically-proven system of parenting except the one you organize by yourself because you know no one else is going to do what needs to be done for you and your children.

As Latter-day Saints, we can recognize that parenthood is part of what is necessary to become like our heavenly parents. Our progress starts by looking for enjoyable ways to help children. Then we form criteria of success just for ourselves, separate from what we want for our children. Then, as we accept our own gradual progress and improvement, we find courage enough to make the difficult decisions parenthood requires. It should be clear that these are rules for progression towards being like our heavenly parents. They have progressed before us and now we are privileged to walk on their paths. As we go, we will undergo the changes and transformations that bring us to the place they want for us. We will have satisfied the learning requirements of parenthood.

Owning a Positive Concept of Childhood

The Savior taught that all human life is of worth and deserves to be nurtured. Those who don't understand this tend either to exalt themselves and exploit others or to abuse themselves and submit to mistreatment. Few of us would admit to being among those who disregard the worth of human life, but it is surprising how many people seem to regard children as in some ways less than human, less worthy of courtesy, regard, respect, and attention than others who are older. Jesus treated children with great respect and tenderness. I especially like the example of this found in the story of the Savior's blessing of the Nephite children. He had been among the Nephites for some time and was ready to leave, but He was so touched by their love of Him and their desires to have Him with them that He stayed to bless them and pray for them. And then, as a final act, He took the children and blessed them one by one, and prayed for them. He asked the parents to look at their children ("Behold your little ones"), and then angels came and ministered to the children in the warmth of the Spirit. Jesus was teaching all who witnessed this that children are of great significance to God.

If we are to instill the truth of the gospel into the hearts of our children, we must believe that children are of inestimable value. It helps to decide that we will always and under every circumstance try to love them, and that our chief interest is in identifying ways to nurture them. If we fail to do this, our children may feel abased by our mistreatment and may learn an incorrect view of their own natures.

Believing that we live in an enlightened and humane time, it is dismaying for us to discover the segments of the human population which are left uncared for or abused. It is fair to say that those children who are always loved and nurtured by their parents without suffering periodic harm or abuse are still in the minority. I am disturbed by the idea that nearly 60 percent of the violent crimes in the United States—including rapes, assaults, and homicides—happen among family members. Also of interest are the results of a periodic inquiry I make of my students at Brigham Young University. When asked if they come from homes where enough love and care was expressed by their parents and siblings, only 54 percent of the students say yes. A full 15 percent of the students polled say they were reared in families where there was no affection and no emotional closeness.

The One who brought the message of an Eternal Father's love for us tried to help all understand that humans are of divine parentage. Children represent all that is possible for human life. They are so important that God knows each one in a unique way. Those who offend His little ones will suffer for it. This view of children can be easily forgotten when children misbehave. When life is stressful or frustrating, it is then that we are most likely to treat children as if they are of little worth to us or anyone. When we are frustrated, children receive the brunt of our anger; both they and we are diminished.

We become better parents when we decide to remember the worth of our children. This means that we will arrange their environment so that they feel secure enough to venture out in life and grow. We do this by spending time with them, paying attention to what they do and say, and letting them know frequently of our love. We all could easily examine the amount of time we take to "behold" our own children, to make our time with them enjoyable, and to love them.

Understanding the Way We Form Relationships with Children

I have on many occasions heard people speak of great activities or wonderful programs that influence children to do good. With few exceptions, it is not the program but the people who share the activity who make a difference. Human progress takes place because of what humans do themselves and also through their relationships with others.

Relationships which stimulate development are filled with special ingredients. Bad relationships can be as destructive as good ones are useful. This is why it is important for us to understand the characteristics of relationships which help children grow.

One important ingredient in good relationships is giving and receiving positive stimulation. There is abundant research showing that children thrive when adults spend time with them in pleasant ways. This satisfying contact seems to stimulate a child's senses and enhances all forms of development. One interesting case study described a moderately retarded girl who visited a foundling home to help feed abandoned infants. While all three babies that she cared for were fed the same food at the same time of day, one grew larger and brighter than the other two. When supervisors wanted to know why, their investigation found that the girl played with the thriving infant one-half hour more each day than the two nonthriving infants. They suggested that growth resulted from the touching, laughing, and hugging which took place. Studies such as this have repeatedly shown that positive attention helps the receiver thrive. It is also true that the giver is helped as well, so it is no surprise that parents grow from giving their children what the children need emotionally.

Another benefit of good relationships is the positive emotional effect they have on us. Whether temporary or lasting, human contact results in increased emotional intensity. When this is positive and enduring, people are motivated to explore, to expand themselves, and to improve. The more positive we make our experiences with the children, the more they will be influenced by us, the more fun we will have, and the better parents we will be.

One way of thinking about progress for parents and children is to consider that a good relationship requires that we develop positive character traits. Some of these, like the ability to love, have patience, and be kind are easily understandable to us. The more we learn these, the better we will get.

In my opinion, the gospel teaches that higher levels of development will occur when we love more deeply and richly, can be more reverent and worshipful, unselfish and charitable, considerate and honest, and more willing to purify thoughts that increase a reception of the Spirit. These are inner qualities, unobservable except when exposed in relationship to other people. Parents and children who learn them succeed in creating close emotional ties. Those who do not learn are lonely and isolated.

It is easy to understand why families exert greater effects on children than any other group. Family relationships are largely inescapable—we are made or broken by our success or failure in them.

Be Adaptable

Because children change as they grow, we must change, grow, and adapt in what we do. When we fail to adapt, we misjudge our children, and what we do may hinder rather than help them. Successful parents observe their children and adapt to new stages of their growth. Through this we can grow, too.

There are some guidelines we can follow to help us make correct adjustments to our children. First, we must to some degree adapt to each of our children based on what we know about them. Some children, as all know, are shy, some are outgoing, some disciplined, and some "go with the flow." These and other characteristics demand that we respond differently, to some degree, to each child. Most of us can do this if we take the time to think about how our children differ from one another.

We also need to observe and interpret changes which take place as each child grows. These may include social, emotional, and mental needs. For example, when children move from childhood to adolescence and have stronger social needs, parents can fail to adapt and keep restrictions tight, while others can adjust to their children's new needs and find ways to help them have positive social experiences.

Second, we should learn about the effects of children's experiences away from the family. Wise parents will not rely on what they went through years earlier but will meet their children's friends and go where they go just to keep themselves informed. If children are often in situations that are hostile to our values we need to adjust sooner rather than later. We must adapt to help our children prepare to find better social reinforcement or to regulate them if their world is hostile to us and them. For example, a realistic appraisal of our children's environment may let us know that we cannot prevent our children from learning about sex. But our investigations tell us that we can either adapt and teach about sex the way we want it done or we can risk our children's learning in ways we do not like.

A third guideline for adapting is based on the idea of anticipation. Having lived longer and traveled paths before them, we can, if we think, anticipate what children will need to know in the future. We can adapt by helping them get ready for something and increase their chances of success. Or, we can wait until they are faced with the task and then respond, perhaps too late. Children progress through levels of school, church, and social relationships. Prior to each move we can identify what they will need to be a success and prepare them with it. As a simple example, parents faced with moving to a new neighborhood took their children for a visit to the new place. They went to the school, met some of the administrators, and looked in the classrooms. They did this two or three times before they actually left their home for good. They felt that the children adjusted well because they were prepared. Anticipating their needs is a useful way to communicate love as children mature. While love is always necessary, the forms we use to express it must change for children to receive it well.

It is through a proper understanding of the worth of children, through happy, stimulating relationships with them, and through successful adaptations to their needs that we mature and enlarge ourselves as parents. Whether by choice or by children's insistence, we discover more about parenthood. As we mature, life gets richer, and parenting gets better. This is the key to progression and happiness. It is to be hoped that all will find fulfillment as parents and have it matched by progress toward all that is good.

3   The Sealing Bond

As we bring our children into the world, they need us and we find them fascinating. A relationship is begun which is the basis for the influence we will have in their lives. As we think about our intention to help children form a close relationship with the Lord and know Him, we should also consider that our relationship with our children may need to be a special kind. Certainly if our children do not or cannot participate in a positive association with us, we will be less able to teach and prepare them. The relationship which brings children to us, we to them, and the entire family together toward the Lord, we might call the sealing bond.

Jesus taught the importance of unity, togetherness, or oneness. It is clear from His teachings that isolation or alienation of human beings from one another is undesirable and that cohesion and involvement are characteristic of people who have lived correctly. This truth is reinforced by ordinances designed to seal families together for shared eternal life.

It is important to understand that a single ordinance does not automatically make a sealing permanent. The ordinance gives us the blessing of sealing if we earn it, by gradually forming a firm attachment to another that cannot be dissolved. An ordinance gives us the power, recognized by God, to earn blessings related to it. The sealing bond between parents and children follows a sealing ordinance if the relationship is properly matured. Parents who activate and maintain this bond will be found sacrificing other things in order to give their children time, companionship, love, and guidance.

A positive bond of attachment between parents and children is the basis of parental influence. This special bond makes children vulnerable to parental guidance and is necessary for children's success. It is the knowledge of being loved which impels children to follow their parents' teachings. No one can say how many times we must show love and concern for any one child, but such shared emotions raise what parents say and do above the ordinary and become their children's recipe for living. A warm and positive relationship activates children's desires to emulate parents. It encourages children to come to us with their mistakes instead of hiding them.

In addition, a positive parent-child attachment is the emotional basis children use to form friendships with others. A secure parent-child bond, for example, may eventually lead to the child's ability to form a deep bond in marriage. When a child does not know loving security, he may be insecure in friendships or later in marriage.

The sealing bond can become the emotional reserve children need to righteously resolve moral dilemmas. It helps them to survive what they face in this world and to keep the spiritual laws in their hearts. Warm ties with parents are the basis children come to use for their relationship with God and for increasing their love for Him. It is harder for children to believe in a loving God and a gospel of love when they live in a non-loving family.

Attachments

Recently behavioral scientists have found there is an early beginning to a secure attachment between parents and children. In one study, for example, fathers who were in the delivery room at the moment of birth subsequently spent more time with their infants than did the fathers who were absent during delivery. As a result of the early father-child involvement, these children performed better later in school. This study, along with others, illustrates the importance of a parent-child relationship called *attachment*.

From birth to twenty months is viewed as the period of time thought to be "critical" for the formation of *secure attachment*. Secure attachment, as contrasted with insecurity, is created when parents allow an infant to move unrestrained, but safely, around the house, adequately care for the child's physical needs (i.e., feeding, dressing, and warmth), give affectionate touches, and talk with and play with the child. Securely attached children suffer "separation distress" in parental absence, but can be comforted and will grow accustomed to new people. They are adventurous but appropriately wary of strangers and new situations. It is important to note that attachment forms for parents as well as for children. Parents who do the foregoing are securely attached and are better able to establish a balance between good child care and their own personal lives.

Insecure attachment is created when caretakers hover too closely, not allowing a child enough freedom of movement, and when basic child care is erratic. When an infant is neglected for periods of time, some think the child learns anger instead of attachment, and fails to thrive. This creates emotional ambivalence. Insecurely attached children often ignore their parents and are either extremely suspicious of others or very unconcerned when they should be concerned. They are less adaptable to new situations, often have extreme emotional reactions, and are difficult to comfort. Parents who are insecurely attached to their children usually over-emphasize their involvement with children and become over-protective or too neglectful. Both of these hurt the children's opportunities for a positive sealing bond with parents.

Involvement Time

As children grow the original attachment begins to take on new forms. Maintaining the affection, of course, is always important; but because children's personalities become more complex, so is the parental responsibility for maintaining a positive relationship. To be successful a variety of child management skills are required that also keep a close parent-child feeling. Two of these seem more important than the others because they balance the management of children and the affectionate bond.

First is the recognition that a secure bond only forms through frequent involvement. With infants, parents take time to give the basic care of feeding, changing diapers, and responding to cries for comfort. As infants grow into toddlers, we let them spend increasing amounts of time alone to climb, crawl, explore, fall, and bump into things. We are glad to escape the confinement early care requires. Then, somehow, a routine of dressing, eating, playing, and sleeping emerges, and children and parents have begun a more lasting schedule.

While this basic care is important, there is more needed. This is the shared time for parents and children to discover each other's personality traits, for parents to find delight in children's growth, and for children to understand their parents' tendencies. A colleague at BYU told me of his experiences with a new child. The bedrooms in their home were all used by other children, so a crib was placed at the foot of the parents' bed. This was something they had not done with their older children. He and his wife often awakened to watch their newest child. His summary of this experience was, "I never imagined all that I was missing. Our baby changed from day to day, it seemed. We have enjoyed this one more than the others."

Hearing his comments, I was reminded of the many people who, because of their busy lives, have missed new growth, missed knowing their children intimately from birth on, and missed knowing of the enjoyment and delight. Quite frequently, these parents (e.g., fathers who are busy in school or away from home when children are young) are never able to create a positive bond with these children. Most misjudgment and mistreatment of children by parents takes place because parents do not have an accurate and full understanding of their children. Then, because parents' success with these children is limited, they desire to be with these children less, and a permanent gap may be created. The gap is widened because these children know less about their absent parents. Later when parents wonder why their children's interests are different from theirs, one reason might be that the children never really knew their parents.

In contrast, what are the consequences for children whose parents seem to find great enjoyment in being with them and spend time noticing all the wonderful things which happen? Children grow secure in the knowledge of their parent's interest, and parents are secure in the knowledge they have of their children's temperaments and personalities.

Our increased awareness about the intimate details of children's lives and characteristics enables us to be more successful in making judgments (from buying Christmas presents to correcting misbehavior). The feelings of competence we get increase our enjoyment of being parents and motivate us to be involved further in our children's lives. This cycle is portrayed in the accompanying diagram.

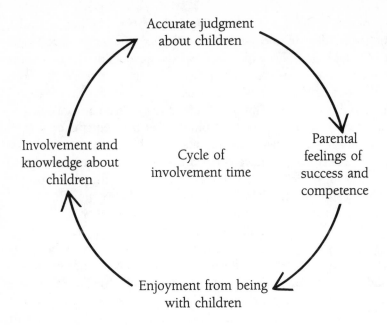

Accurate judgment
about children

Involvement and
knowledge about
children

Cycle of
involvement time

Parental
feelings of
success and
competence

Enjoyment from being
with children

Notice Each Child's Temperament

Many parents report they are better able to succeed with and
enjoy later-born children because they did not know what to look
for while their older children were maturing. They feel they "practiced"
on their oldest. We can improve our chances for success if we take
the time to learn about the nature of a child's temperament. Each
child will be different, but each can be understood in terms of the
eight temperament qualities shown in table 3.1 (taken from A. Thomas
and S. Chess, *Temperament and Development* [New York: Brun-
ner/Mazel, 1977]).

Table 3.1
Children's Temperaments

Temperament Quality	Description
Activity Level	The amount of physical movement a child displays.
Rhythmicity	Whether the child's biological functions (e.g., eating habits) are regular or irregular.
Approach or Withdrawal	A child's initial reaction to something new may be to approach it positively or withdraw from it.
Adaptability	A child may be able to adapt well to different situations or he/she may not adjust well and may be troubled.
Intensity of Reaction	This is a measure of a child's energy level. Loud, intense reactions suggest high energy levels. This will affect the ability to work and perform later on.
Responsiveness and Distractability	Children vary in the amount of sensation they must have in order to react. Some are affected by small amounts of stimulus (e.g., noise), and others seem to ignore much more. Highly responsive children are more impulsive and have difficulty in concentrating.
Quality of Mood	This is the proportion of happy and friendly to unhappy and unfriendly behavior. Moods in young children often continue into adulthood.
Attention Span and Persistence	The length of time activities are maintained and the tolerance children have for difficult tasks. Children high in persistence will finish things (reading a book). Children low in persistence will seldom continue on any project.

Knowing children's temperaments can help us make more accurate judgments about them. We can also better predict what traits will emerge in our children's personalities later on in life and guide them along the way.

Besides participating in the involvement cycle, parents strengthen the sealing bond with children through activities that teach. A young child is curious a large part of the time and when curiosity is stimulated by parents, the bond between children is strengthened. Some parents think teaching must take the form of structured times where things like the alphabet and numbers are taught. While this might be useful, the teaching suggested here for young children (under the age of four) is to explain their environment to them. It is not only important what we teach, it is active parental involvement in teaching that is important. It is through parents talking, showing, playing, listening, and explaining that children begin to rely on parents' ideas and explanations. If a parent explains how a toy works, for example, and the child finds it is true, the child also expects parents to be trustworthy. This is deepened through many such experiences. Involved parents take this for granted, but there is clear and consistent support for the idea that such "trusting" attitudes and experiences early in children's lives are related to successful parent-child relationships later on.

The Magic of Childhood Language

A new world opens when our children have learned language skills and begin to reason with words. Our task is a bit more difficult now, but it is more fun in some ways, too. This period (age four to eleven) is as important as any other time in a child's life, and in some ways it is more so. Let's suppose that there is free and frequent exchange of affection and warmth. What can be done with language to add to the developing bond between us and our children?

For instance, this is a period of time that children learn conversation skills. The amount they talk, what they talk to parents about, and when they do it is all established by age twelve. To some extent, we shape a child's world through our use of language. Linguists have found, for instance, that children learn to use language in order to communicate with their parents and will learn the style of language used by their parents. Positive language patterns which children will learn include the following:

1. Listening quietly
2. Listening actively (asking questions)
3. No interruptions while someone is speaking
4. Using "I" language (e.g., "I think" or "I hope")
5. Praise and encouragement instead of pessimism

Two points warrant our attention. First, the words we use influence how we think and act. If we wish our children to accept the gospel, we must teach them a gospel vocabulary. Second, children will emulate the language styles of their parents. Language, of course, is the substance of our conversations, and time spent between parents and children talking is extremely valuable. If we want a good conversational relationship, we can create it when children are young. Because communication is the medicine we use to reinforce the attachment bond throughout life, while the children are young and unsure, we can do a few things to make our communication more effective. These are shown in table 3.2.

The importance of open conversation between parents and children should not be underestimated. It is the one condition which consistently appears in family research as the reason for "close" families. Communication can be improved when parents use their family organization to increase children's involvement. Some of these include discussions of family plans, such as decisions about new purchases and vacations. In addition, you may wish to notice what prevents conversations from taking place. Television, for example, is watched an average of four and a half hours each day in American families. Unless you regulate the amount of TV watching, your children will view twenty-seven thousand hours of televised communication by the time they are eighteen years old.

Parents can use language to "give children a place" in the family by asking each child to share in the work and by focusing on the talents and talking about traits which make each child unique. One child will be neat and organized, another interested in music, another successful in sports, and so forth.

Table 3.2
Making Communication with Children More Effective

Conversation Skills	Effects for Children	Consequences
Listening and encouraging children to talk	Children gain a sense of comfort about talking to you about any topic they wish. You become approachable.	When children are faced with questions (e.g., about sex) or have problems, they will more easily come to you rather than avoid you because they think you cannot understand.
Talking to children (explaining)	Children benefit from suggestions, knowing reasons for things and how to apply what you tell them.	Children can develop goal-oriented behavior because they understand the reasons or explanations for things. They will be more calm because they understand things better.
Telling stories	Children are attracted by stories. They form attitudes about moral values and retain pleasant memories.	Stories help children develop moral values, develop a sense of humor, and develop a sense of imagination and fantasy.
What you talk about	What you emphasize shapes a child's perceptual make-up. If you focus on nature, they will learn that. If you talk about personal things (i.e., your feelings) they will learn that. If you discuss religious topics they will learn and understand that, too.	A child's ideas about himself, other people, careers, work habits, religion, and similar topics all come from what you talk about. These influence the choices a child will make later on.
When you do it	A child will learn to use conversation when you do (for example, talking over problems instead of getting angry, talking about experiences when they come home, and keeping you informed of their whereabouts).	Conversation is an effective tool to promote and maintain friendships, family relationships, and marriage. Your children can be more successful in these areas by learning when to use conversation skills in many situations.

Expressing Confidence in Our Young Children

Most parents wisely and gradually do all the foregoing as children grow and mature. But there is one thing that many do not do, even though it keeps a good relationship as children move into adolescence. Many of us fail through communication to let our children know that we believe in them.

As children begin to spread their social wings, they begin to encounter increasing amounts of uncertainty. It is understandable that they would want the companionship of friends who share their feelings. Friends are not enough, however, to help children believe in themselves. Most of us realize that children who continue to persist and who try new experiences are those who believe in their own abilities. But we often forget that children's belief in themselves usually comes from their parents' confidence in them.

Children know that parents know them well. When parents express belief in their children, encourage them to do well, praise good performance, and uplift them in times of discouragement, children gradually acquire confidence in themselves. This belief is also referred to as achievement motivation or self-esteem, but whatever it is called, it is created within children by their parents. We can never underestimate the power of the praise that we give or the conversations that we have with our children about their successes.

The sealing bond between us and our children is strengthened when we expose children to varieties of new and good experiences and help them feel our joy in them as they participate. If we consistently and warmly share with them and talk together, they will learn that they are more important to us than any particular achievement. Then, when we express our positive impressions of their efforts, they know we believe in them.

Acceptance for Preteens

Children are afraid when we yell, criticize, overcontrol, or neglect. Too much of this behavior can create permanent fearfulness and a sense of perpetual failure in a child. And even the best of us can too often withdraw confidence and warmth when children fail without realizing that failure may signal a greater need for our support than any success would.

It is not so difficult to let our children know that we will care for them regardless of what they do. Our children are a permanent part of us and cannot be severed from us just because they do wrong or make mistakes. They are gloriously wise parents who know that children need them in times of stress, times of failure, and times of wrongdoing. Even if the children's actions are embarrassing, children are never free to not need their parents.

One father described a little league baseball game in which he learned something about loving and believing in children. Emotions were intense because the score was close. Parents were cheering their sons, moaning at inadequacy, yelling their disagreements at the umpires. In the midst of this, the father's son walked out of the dugout and selected a batting helmet and a bat. He took a few practice swings and waited his turn. The boy at bat walked, filling the bases. A hit of any kind would tie the score and an "out" would end the game. The boy was tight-lipped and grim as he strode to the plate. The parents of players on his team cheered encouragement: "You can do it." "Get a hit." "A hit's a run." His coaches joined the chorus of voices.

In the lull before the first pitch, the boy turned and looked into the stands. His father yelled out to him, "I don't care if you strike out. It's all right if you don't get a hit." At first everyone laughed at the strangeness of the comments, but then the other parents began to react to this different message, and they quieted. A flicker of a smile appeared on the boy's face as he turned to the pitcher. He had received the message: "Dad is there; I am here. And it does not matter if I fail. We'll still be together." The boy knew that *he* was more important to his father than what he *did* as a baseball player. Incidentally, the son, I was told, hit the ball and won the game for his team.

The Age of Expectation and Emotional Support

Family life is most complex when our children are of differing ages, especially if some of them are adolescents. Adolescent children bring us particular challenges because of what they undergo in order to become adults. Children this age in our culture usually try to establish a sense of increasing freedom from authority or other restrictions. Sometimes they are responsible enough to live a self-determined life, but many want fewer restrictions than they still need.

Adolescents also are confronted with important decisions concerning careers, religious values, friends, and money. These decisions require us to participate with our adolescent children in conversations of increased importance. As we face the necessity of understanding the complex needs of a teenager, the teenager is busy extending relationships to people outside the family and spending increasing amounts of time away from home. In our society, associating with groups of adolescents is the primary way our children separate themselves from us and become independent. For this reason, our children's successful friendships with good people are important to us. Some groups, as we all know, encourage our children to separate from us in desirable ways; other groups are not so positive in their effects. In any event, social success with friends, dates, and even other adults is important, and adolescents face considerable pressures in this regard.

It is often a delicate task to balance a child's need for increased freedom with the maintenance of our parent-child bond. Further, the working out of each developmental task can require us to adapt how we relate to each other. But if we study families that succeed in helping children to accomplish all these tasks and achieve active independence with a warm bond intact, we find a common pattern: these adolescents receive sustained emotional support from parents.

Giving emotional support does not necessarily mean agreeing with everything children do or say. It does not mean giving permission to do whatever children want to do, nor does it mean showing casual amusement with their dilemmas or with the "wild oats" they sow. Sometimes emotional support is active—responding, guiding, encouraging. Other times it is passive—quietly understanding and accepting children's emotions, for instance. We must appropriately balance our influence. If we are too involved, we will communicate control, creating resentment and possibly delaying or preventing our children's independence. Too little involvement, however, can have the same result, as children flounder and become angry at us.

This obviously requires skill on our part. We can begin by first gathering information before we try to respond to our children's needs. Once we have enough information to accurately evaluate a situation and are committed to giving emotional support, we can decide whether active or passive support is best. Some common situations and possible helpful parental responses are described in table 3.3.

Table 3.3
Emotional Support with Adolescent Children

Situations	Active Emotional Support	Passive Emotional Support
1. A child is angry at friends and takes it out on the parents.	After calmly responding to the outburst, inquire about what experience may have preceded it.	Listen carefully without getting angry at the child's unfair disrespect. The anger has little to do with the parents, even though the child is directing it at them.
2. A child is participating in activities which have value to the child.	Interested attendance and shared conversation show care and emotional support.	Do not be passive.
3. A child fails to follow a family rule (e.g., curfew).	Increase positive warmth and love, especially at the time it is discovered that the rule has been violated. After becoming informed about the reasons, ask the child what he/she intends to do next time.	Withhold extreme expressions of anger and frustration. Focus on objective of helping the child become more responsible.
4. A child is overly involved with a boyfriend or girlfriend.	Show warmth and increase the number of positive family activities. Work to create a pleasant and open channel of communication. Show affection and care. If your child cannot manage an uncontrolled relationship, consider (1) restricting him, (2) removing him from the situation.	Avoid condemning your child or your child's friend. Condemnation and criticism will force your child to choose sides. Also avoid involving the friend in many family activities in order to try to "get to know" the friend.

5. A child has unhappy social experiences like exclusion or conflict.	Reinforce your concern and care while searching for awareness that will lead to more success. Help your child avoid isolation. Show support by attention.	Avoid taking sides when a child complains. It is generally best to not intervene in children's problems with peers except to other adults who might help, and this only as a last resort.
6. A child suddenly behaves erratically, shows unusual mood changes, and changes performance levels dramatically.	Quickly gather information about your child's friends, activities, and relationships with teachers and leaders. Check for involvement with chemical substances, immoral behavior, or emotional crises. (a) Frequently reinforce your love and care for the child. (b) Consider restricting the child's activities after exploring reasons. (c) Consider a change of environment. (d) Encourage the child to accept responsibility for what is done to solve the problem.	Do not be passive.
7. A child talks about ideas or values which conflict with your own.	Actively support opportunities to learn about the ideas or values and show support while doing so. Ask your child to learn more with you. Ask your child to talk about the attitude and then ask if he or she will respectfully hear you. Encourage your child to participate in hearing about what you value.	Avoid argumentation and conflict. It will not change a child's opinion. Calmness shows confidence in what you believe.

If we want to maintain the ties that will bless and strengthen our children, we will never withhold our emotional support from them. If, for instance, a child is late coming home, we will welcome him and discuss lateness the next day. We will show love even if we are anxious. We will express stern concern if wrong is being done, so that the child will know we are not indifferent. If a child confesses a wrongdoing, we will tell him of our love before stating the rules. We will notice our children's moods and invite conversations that help us understand. We will respect a child's needs and desires while encouraging him.

We can show our support by teaching children how to make decisions and by sharing decisions with them. We can say, "What do you think you will do?" "What are your plans tonight?" "Let's discuss this situation to find what is best for you." Further, we can remind children that responsibility must increase as freedom does and help them see this happening in their lives. This is accomplished when we ask them about what they will do, why they will do it, and who makes the decisions that affect what they do. They can learn that their responsible behavior allows us to trust them and to decrease our control over their lives.

Finally, we must never underestimate the importance of the emotional support shown in simply talking with our children. Conversations are usually easy to create when we pay attention to what our children are doing and invite them to be with us. If open communication is our family style, children's willingness to talk to us is often a barometer of the way they evaluate themselves. Talking or silence that varies from the usual can mean a child is wrestling with some momentary or long-standing difficulty. If we are concerned, we should not try to get them to talk or reveal the problem first. It is best to reinforce the parent-child relationship by showing emotional support through gestures of care or in statements of support and confidence. If we express our support first, showing respect for their privacy, and listen with interest to what they say, we will usually succeed in creating a climate in which they can talk and in maintaining a close attachment to our children throughout their adolescence.

In most cases a warm attachment maintained between parents and children from birth through adolescence will ensure a lifetime of unity, a sealing bond. If we create this emotional base for our children, they will follow after us, know our ways, and desire to please us. They will accept the principles we teach them, and these will later guide them with their children, perpetuating the laws they have learned in their hearts.

4   Rules and Relationships

It has been said that obedience to the laws of God is the first law of heaven. It is easy to assume this statement only reflects the need to comply and the benefits of complying with righteous law. The word *obedience* should not be mistaken for conformity. Obedience requires the exercise of free agency because we know the good that will come from obeying. In contrast, conformity is compliance because of pressure to do so. To be truly obedient, a person must go beyond merely conforming. The first law of heaven includes free agency, knowledge about God's laws, and the motivation to live them.

We face a dilemma concerning obedience as we try to teach our children about God and to obey Him. There are times when we must "make" children comply. If that is all we do, however, we know this removes their freedom because of our pressure on them. On the other hand, if they have too little pressure from us, they may not comply at all. How then do we motivate them to choose to obey God's commandments?

I suggest we motivate them by the way we adapt our approach to family rules and the way we increase children's sense of agency by teaching them to participate in a relationship with us. An example of this is found in the way God formed a relationship with Israel.

When the Israelites left Egypt, the years of slavery had made them excessively dependent on authority. Like children, they took their problems to Moses instead of trying to solve them themselves. When they were left for forty days without Moses to lead them, they were unable to follow the laws the Lord had already given them. Therefore, in place of the higher spiritual laws he had intended for them, the Lord, through Moses, provided the Israelites with a set of prescriptions which applied to very specific situations. This collection of rules, which came to be known as the law of Moses, referred to a person's actions rather than the inner world of his thoughts and motives.

The effects of this set of laws can be observed in the Old Testament and Book of Mormon peoples. The Jewish culture formed around the study, teaching, refinement, and enforcement of law. Children became literate in order to know about the law. Their first readings and writings were the Talmud, Torah, or scholarly writings designed to interpret the laws. Theirs became a society where religious law was also civil law. Social status ordinarily achieved through education and wealth was, in Hebrew society, also determined by one's mastery of the law through study and application.

Because of the law's emphasis on external behavior, it was easy to judge other people exactly by what they did or did not do. It is fairly easy to understand the pressures this placed on people. The judgment of others often prevented violations of the law, but because the law focused on external actions, one could avoid being judged by others by appearing to conform with the law even if private acts were not compliant. This led to attempts by some segments of society to seek positions, for example, in the higher seats of their synagogue (Luke 11:43), to extol their own marvelous compliance to the law and condemn others for their inadequacy (Luke 18:10-13), and to engage in hypocrisy in order to avoid judgment.

A successful person in that day and culture was one who conformed to the law or appeared to conform to the law. It was often not possible to tell the difference. People became more concerned about conformity and others' judgment than any other ideal. This is the situation Jesus found as He entered His ministry among these people.

In contrast to the religion of the Jews at the time of His birth, the Savior's gospel of love introduced the Holy Ghost, which speaks to the spiritual part of us. The gospel had a different effect on those who learned and lived it than did the law of Moses. Jesus introduced the concept of righteousness. This proposed that conformity to the rule of law by others' judgment should no longer be pursued as the final objective of people who wished to be good people. Instead, according to the Savior, a righteous person was to reflect on thoughts, intentions, and desires to do all things (including obeying the law) in honesty, love, and peace of mind. These conditions are those which make people better and help us grow to higher levels of righteousness.

In the Savior's fulfillment of the old set of rules, He provided the way for us to form a spiritual relationship with Him. Through this relationship, we are to sense the correctness of principles, apply them on our own, and benefit from the development we create in ourselves. It is not only the concepts or the ideas in the gospel that create this growth. It is also, and perhaps most important, this ongoing spiritual association with Him.

It is clear that lower and higher laws exist, and our spiritual growth depends on our ability to progress from one to the other. This spiritual growth to higher levels of human development could be expected for us as we live the law of the gospel, which fulfilled the law of Moses. Jehovah, who gave the higher law to His children on several occasions, gave it again to mankind at the time of His earthly life. Even then there was not a widespread sustained success at living it, as shown by the great apostasy. This higher law of the inner spirit was presented to us in more modern times with the promise that it would not be removed. It is now up to us to use it and teach it to our children. From all this, we can conclude that His laws are given for our development. And that as we grow we do so from one level to another. Further, for complete benefit, a law we live by must match our level of maturity.

The examples of Hebrew people show how we can be affected by the types of laws which govern us. The examples can be applied to what we do as parents. If, for example, exclusive attention is drawn to external behavior (e.g., "Is your work done?" "Stop acting that way!") and rules are formed to regulate it, children may acquire only the qualities similar to many Pharisees. If we increase our focus to include internal conditions where the gospel suggests we should, we can set the stage for children to live consistently according to an inner law. If we adjust what we do and gradually raise our family laws to higher levels as children mature and adapt them to children's unique qualities, the possible benefits to them are even improved.

Children and Their Rules

Any regular event is a family rule. It may be informal, like a family tradition which we do without speaking much about it, or formal, like getting dressed before breakfast. To a child anything which is repeated frequently enough will become a rule. Informal rules seem to evolve as a natural part of family living. Formal rules are taught to children and enforced by positive reward or punishment. There is no such thing as a family without rules. There is only a difference in the number of informal rules compared to formal rules. More informal rules lead to a more permissive situation. More formal rules create a more strict parental style. This chapter is concerned with the way children think about formal rules and the way parents can adapt these rules into principles in order to constructively help children develop.

Behavioral scientists have studied children's concept of rules and have concluded that (1) the concept children have about rules changes as they mature, and (2) children's acceptance of parental authority depends on whether parents correctly match their use of rules to a child's stage of development. This suggests that for any plan of discipline to succeed, parents need to understand the stages of rule development, learn how to recognize them, and be able to adapt them to a child's individual level of maturity.

It is generally accepted that prior to three and a half years of age, a child either has no concept of formal rules or has a very rudimentary notion about what they are. Parents can, by strict observance, teach young children to avoid touching something or avoid going into some restricted place, but these actions are more like responses to a stimulus than following a rule. Young children are influenced by the things they see, hear, smell, touch, and taste. They are usually curious and do whatever appears to be of interest at the time. Their interests are not of long duration either, so for the most part, parents need not worry about formal rules during the first years of a child's life.

My wife has usually allowed our children great amounts of freedom to roam and explore in the house. Drawers or cupboards that are off-limits were tied shut. I received a good impression one day of the way children under three think about rules. Our young son, a toddler, climbed inside the pots-and-pans cupboard and threw them out on the floor, enjoying the clanging sounds. I removed him from that affair, and before I finished gathering the pans, I heard him on the dining room table, throwing things off of it. I lifted him from the table and began lifting the chairs up to prevent him from climbing up again. Before I could finish this, I heard noises from my home office and quickly went to see; I found him on my desk throwing books and papers off. I felt as though a good spanking would help me feel better. But by then I had learned it wouldn't have made much difference to him, so I hugged him and gave him a new toy. He never repeated the wrong action. Attempts to create formal rules to regulate children this age often end in failure unless we are willing to employ restrictive conditions.

From four years to nine, a child forms a concept of formal rules that is fairly rigid and inflexible. Once a rule is impressed on them, children expect and benefit from consistent application of rules. Those rules are the way children organize their concept of the world, and they want and need some regularity which they can use to predict what will happen to them. These may include family routines (e.g., "get up, make your bed, get dressed, come to breakfast"). Rules of conduct (e.g., how to answer the telephone) may also be created which increase their satisfaction and improve their performance. Other examples of these rules include activities like responding to a knock on the door and behaving properly in church.

One could go to any school playground and see the inflexible way children first think about formal rules. If children learn the rules of four square (a game using a bouncing ball), they will insist these rules be followed the same way each time it is played. Any attempt to adjust the rules is met with argument and anger. "This is the way we do it," a child will say, as if no other possibilities exist. Most parents can also think of times when they formed a rule and then had to adjust it. The children most frustrated by this are those ages four through nine. If we are not consistent in what we do and what we expect of them, children are less secure. Flagrant inconsistency can create emotions that stimulate erratic behavior. Many children with highly inconsistent parents learn to use misbehavior to test the consistency of the rules, and consequently they become more difficult to manage.

From age nine to twelve (recognize that many children will vary from these age ranges), children show an inclination to adapt rules.

They will do so to fit special circumstances like playing baseball with only eight players. Further, they show an ability to negotiate rules with others with a fine sense of fairness. Adapting, however, usually requires some explanation, and so children begin to search for reasons which can satisfy this need. If without good reason parents adapt rules which have previously been consistently applied, children will be more suspicious, even cynical, about parental authority. Most parents adjust to this stage by increasing the amount of conversation about rules, giving reasons why they should be followed or adjusted.

In the last stage of child development, beginning around age thirteen, children display some of the characteristics of earlier years, but in addition and more important, they have the ability to formulate rules themselves to fit their own purposes. They will, for example, usually display a fixed attitude about some rules (e.g., those for family meals), while displaying some unwillingness to follow other rules, wanting to construct their own. This variety is one reason why many adolescent children seem to confuse and frustrate their parents. It is difficult to know which attitude to apply to any rule. Many parents feel as if they must now start over again and rethink every rule they have established. Some react by stabilizing their rules, refusing to adapt any. Others relax too many as a result of children's pressure to do so. Most of us face the dilemma of not knowing when to adjust and when not to.

Matching Your Strategies to Children's Stages of Growth

One progression principle is based on the idea that as our children mature, we must adapt our treatment of them to best help them succeed. It is often the case that our approach fails to match what children feel within themselves and they are reluctant to accept what we ask of them. There are, of course, times when parents must insist on obedience to a rule even when children are less than happy about doing so. Most of the time, however, parental problems with children occur because of our failure to even try to adapt successfully. Some common examples include attempting to structure and harshly enforce rules with very young children, lacking regularity in teaching or enforcing rules, enforcing too many or too few rules, and attempting to enforce rules for older children the same way we do for younger children.

Since our object is to transmit to the lives of our children the law we live, it makes sense to do what will be understood by them. This does not mean they will always like or agree with what we do, but if we match our approach to their state of readiness, they will better understand. If they can understand, they will more likely accept and live what they learn.

Children's readiness about rules can be identified in the normal course of maturation. After they first learn and appreciate formal rules, they appear to naturally move to greater flexibility. This does not mean all will sometimes obey and sometimes not (although most do that anyway). It means that their minds are gradually learning how to transform a rule for a specific situation into a principle of conduct that can be applied in several situations. When they learn to apply a rule in many different forms and places, it has become a principle and is no longer just a rule. (See table 4.1.)

Table 4.1
Parental Authority and
Development of Children's Concepts About Rules

Parental authority and children's authority are now equal in importance	4. Rules become principles which children apply by themselves based on (1) previous rules they have learned and (2) the requirements of a new situation
Diminished parental authority, allowing children to adapt some rules to suit themselves	3. Children begin to adapt rules to satisfy new situations
High levels of parental authority to which children reach	2. Children gain a fixed application of rules
Little parental authority except as caretakers and teachers	1. Children experiment

If we are to succeed at matching our treatment of rules to our children's changing levels of maturity, we must take both our use of authority and their ideas about rules into account. By doing this gradually, we can evolve a family plan that will allow us to guide our children toward successful and righteous lives. A proposal for doing this can be seen in table 4.2.

The Governing Relationship: How Rules Become Principles

Earlier in this chapter I suggested that we ordinarily start children with specific rules for behavior in a specific action. In this process, we impose considerable authority in order to govern them. For children to develop a sense of freedom that permits obedience, however, they must be able to gradually learn how to act without much authority imposed and be able to think more thoroughly and adapt rules to fit several situations. Being able to use more information in making one's own decisions is the application of a principle of conduct rather than an application of a rule. As parents, we need something which gradually changes us from the position of enforcer of rules to a teacher of principles for living. This is done in the establishment of a positive parent-child relationship which emphasizes relations with one another instead of reward or punishment of children.

After we have taken our children from birth to adolescence, one could feel we have already formed a relationship with them. We have to some extent, but it is usually a relationship of a parent authority to a subordinate child.

To illustrate, let's consider the event of "coming home." When children are very young we know they do not know much about time or the need to pay attention to schedules, so we usually don't let them stray very far, go get them when we want them, and seldom punish them if they are late. When they are older we usually want them in "before dark," "in time for dinner," or other similar times. We expect them to pay attention to time and will impose some disciplinary measure if they are late. Later, when they are involved in little league games, dance practice, or piano lessons, we usually begin to adjust; for example, we delay dinner for them. Still later, during adolescence they are faced with friends, dates, movie schedules, parties, games and the like. The specific rules of earlier times do not apply, because deciding the time they come home is

Table 4.2
Parental Strategies and Children's Stages of Development

	What Parents Can Do	Children's Stage
Stage 1 (0-3½)	This is a time for parents to include children in informal rules (routines) while employing basic care and preventing harm.	Children have limited concepts of rules. They respond to cues from their environment, are curious, distractable, influenced by their moods, and think of life as accomplishing basic tasks of coordinating their sense.
Stage 2 (4-9)	Identify a few basic rules in the family and teach them by showing what is expected. Consistently follow-through and reinforce success by positive consequences and failure by new efforts to perform. In order to get a few good rules fully taught, emphasize successful accomplishment more than failure.	Children understand that rules can be formed for what they do (e.g., chores) and how they act (e.g., be polite). They have a rigid concept of rules and tend to prefer that life be somewhat organized and predictable.
Stage 3 (10-12)	Increase your explanations and reasons for your instructions. Expect children to try to negotiate with you. Begin to de-emphasize formal rules in favor of clarity about what to do in specific situations.	Children begin to adapt the rules to fit their circumstances. Therefore, they expect that rules and their enforcement should be reasonably logical and understandable. They will follow rules that are enforced and will test to see which rules do not have to be followed.
Stage 4 (13-18)	Parents can replace the emphasis on formal rules with the creation of a positive parent-child relationship. This allows discussion of what is best in a given situation, clarifies what each expects, allows children a role in governing themselves, and helps parents and children learn the emotional consequences of what each does.	Children can adapt rules to many different circumstances, but need help to know how to be consistent in some and flexible in others. This works best when formal rules are de-emphasized and children's conduct is regulated through their relationship with parents.

now more complex. We must find a way to help our children learn and apply a principle (taking everything into consideration) that was once a rule.

Most of the time we read about child discipline which emphasizes ways to enforce rules in order to manage what children do. We often give less appreciation to the extraordinary influence of the relationship between parents and children. If the relationship has the proper ingredients, it is much more effective in teaching children to correctly apply principles than any system of rules we could devise. If children fail to participate successfully in such a relationship at the right time, more often they will see life as a set of rules imposed by some authority. To create any sense of comfort, some will remove themselves from sources of authority like church and schools and live in frustration. Others will seek comfort by overconforming and will require someone to tell them what to do before they will act at all.

We can teach our children what a good relationship is and ask them to participate in it. I tell mine that a good relationship is made up of several things: First, each person is considered equally important even though he may act different from another person. Parents may have wisdom that comes from great experience and have to act responsibly for their family. Children's ideas are based on their experience and their ideas are different as a result, but of equal importance. Second, a good relationship is characterized by frequent communication in which we tell each other of our feelings and ideas and keep each informed about our activites. (This means specifically that we will tell each other our plans and inform one another if those plans change.)

Third, a good relationship has freedom and trust in it. We accomplish this as parents and children by saying what we will do, and doing what we say. Fourth, a good relationship is the measure of our individual actions. That is, we will evaluate what we each do in terms of how it affects our relationship. When we are responsible, the relationship works well. When we are not, for one reason or another, the relationship suffers. Last, a governing relationship is based on an encouraging love that is expressed to each other. This, of course, reinforces the value and the influence of the relationship on us.

I tell each of my children when they reach adolescence that they can choose between having a good relationship with their mother and me or they can have a lot of rules. I am sure they don't know much about a relationship at the time, but they do know about rules and don't like them. They all have chosen the "good" relationship. They are informed about the characteristics described above and we talk about examples of them. We try to exemplify the parts of the relationship in order to set an example. We assume it takes quite a while for children to learn how to succeed in this relationship, and we see that as our goal for them before they leave home.

One day a woman stopped me as I was leaving a little league baseball game and in exasperation said, "My daughter tells me you don't have any curfews for your children." "That's right," I informed her, "with one exception. We expect our children to be home by 12:00 on Saturday night." She told me of her frustration with her daughter who resisted their curfews. Her daughter had asked mine what we did, and after finding out, she went home and used it as leverage against her parents. "Well," I said, "don't use me as an example. Do what you think best." She calmed a bit and asked me to explain how we could control our children without a rule to make them come home on time. I explained to her that we had the practice of this relationship, and when our children went out for an evening, we talked about their plans and they decided when they would come home. "What if they didn't come home when they agreed?" she asked. "I expect them to tell me of their change of plans," I answered. "Do they come home when they say?" was the next question. "Usually," I told her. "Sometimes they will run into something and be later than planned." "Do they call?" she asked. "Yes, almost always, unless it is not possible." Then she asked the clinching question. "Why do they?" she wanted to know. "Because they want to do what they say and they value our relationship. We have talked about what happens if one person can't be trusted."

I told her of a time when one of my daughters didn't come home at the agreed-upon time. I explained how that child was asked if she wanted to destroy the trust between us. After we discussed it, we worked out another evening when this girl could go out again in order to practice until she "got it right." I explained that we ask our children to be in before midnight on Saturdays, because as a religious family we felt the Sabbath day began at midnight. Equally important, however, was the idea that we wanted each of our children to be faced with something they would have to defend in front of their friends. We think if our children can inform their friends of this schedule and stick to it, they will be able to be loyal to other principles such as the Word of Wisdom or honesty when opportunities are presented to misuse them.

One episode with this idea occurred with a son who is somewhat quiet but wonderfully willing to please. We were concerned that he would not be able to tell his friends that if he went with them, they must agree to have him back by midnight. It was especially difficult because at the beginning he was not old enough to drive. When he first went with his friends they did not make it back on time, and of course neither did he. He was apologetic and gave what sounded like good explanations. We encouraged him to keep trying, asking him what he told his friends before going out and what he did in order to get them to come home. This went on for four or five such evenings. Each time he was getting better, but still hadn't made it in on time. One night, because a promised ride failed to materialize, he was unusually late. He stopped in our bedroom and after telling us he was home (keeping us informed), he was filled with self-recrimination and said, "You can ground me, Dad." I told him we would talk about it later and we did.

The next day we discussed the whole matter again (talking and listening to each other). I gave him our reasons as parents for the difficulties he faced with his friends. At the conclusion, he asked if I was going to ground him. "No, but we're going to keep working on it until we get it," I replied. I told him of my love for him and my sympathy for how hard it was and that I was proud of him for working at it. I told him the consequences of his actions for me. I have learned that he has since told his friends that he has a deal with his dad and he wants to keep it. They have helped him keep his deal with me, and of course, I think he is a great son for doing that.

I have used this example to show how the governing relationship works. First, it helps children transform rules into principles and enables parents to exert indirect but strong influence on their children. As parents we could think of the Saturday night rule only as a rule that prescribes how children should act at that exact time. We want them, however, to learn to participate in a relationship with us that results in knowing more information about coming in before midnight. Second, this example illustrates that conversation and renewed efforts to improve are good ways of helping children apply the principles. It takes time for a child to truly understand something and even more to arrange conditions with his friends. Eventually his understanding about the correctness of the idea will motivate him without his parents being there. In my experience it is the only effective way to teach a principle of conduct, because punishment or parental anger will, if they work at all, only work when parents are closely supervising. Last, this example shows how parents can use a situation to teach children how to perform in a relationship that gives them part of the freedom and responsibility to govern themselves. We talked openly. We encouraged each other. As his father, my attention and involvement let him know I cared about this matter; I was not going to impose punishment, but I was not going to simply let it pass. At this point, he seems to care about it also.

I have my limitations as a parent, as most do, and am not through with the challenges that will certainly come my way, so I do not want to hold myself as the example for everyone else to follow. Rather I think it is possible for every parent to create a governing relationship that fits his or her style and works well. The best part of this relationship, though, is that it inspires parents to be the best they can. The children will catch all of our mistakes if we fail to fulfill our part. Perhaps it is a nice way of governing us as well as our children.

5   Right and Wrong

Heavenly Father is the author of all that brings happiness. Yet children do not automatically know this nor do they naturally obey His laws which bring happiness. The discovery of God's love for us, His children, and the motivation to obey Him can come from a clear knowledge of what is right and what is wrong.

Traditional child-rearing practices focus on children's wrong behavior and suggest the use of a variety of punishments. Parents mistakenly assume that punishment is sufficient to teach children to avoid doing what is wrong, but it is as necessary for us to help children learn and do what is right. The real power of the gospel of Jesus Christ, for example, lies in its description of what is right to do, which also enables us to know what is wrong. Through the experience of happiness from doing right and the guilt and shame from doing wrong, our children find for themselves that God is the one who gives us the way to have a fulness of joy. This discovery increases children's love for God and motivates them to be like Him.

The gospel message brought by the Savior suggests that success for mortals was to be measured by increased righteousness. Our Heavenly Father and Jesus were held up as examples of what we were to learn and eventually become like. Many, like the Pharisees who used observance of the law to obtain high positions, predictably rejected this message because it brought equality to mankind. Anyone could become better or more righteous by doing what was right which promotes spiritual development, and by resisting what was wrong, which impairs human progress. The new law was one of the heart.

Scriptural record shows that the Savior considered repentance and forgiveness to be important because they enable people to stop doing wrong and begin doing right again. Many of the Pharisees were shocked at His willingness to forgive sin, because a "sinner" was someone in a very low social position and, to them, could not easily be forgiven. On one occasion (Luke 7), a woman followed Jesus into a Pharisee's home, anointed Him, washed His feet with her tears, and wiped them with her long beautiful hair. Simon the Pharisee, unmoved by this display, reasoned that "if Jesus were a prophet, He would know the woman was a sinner" and therefore He should have sent her away. Instead, Jesus taught Simon about love and said about the woman, "Her sins, which are many, are forgiven; for she loved much" (verse 47). Pointing out that the woman must have received forgiveness through repentance and baptism, Elder Bruce R. McConkie says that Jesus was in effect saying: "Her gratitude knows no bounds and her love is beyond measure for she was forgiven of much. Had she been forgiven of but few sins, she would not have loved me so intensely." (*Doctrinal New Testament Commentary*, vol. 1 [Bookcraft, 1965], p. 265.)

Loving much is a way to achieve forgiveness. It is right, for it is a way to progress and be a better person. Instead of appreciating the tenderness and warmth of the moment, those who sat at dinner reasoned about whether the law had been satisfied. They questioned Jesus' conformity to it by saying within themselves, "Who is this that forgiveth sins also?" Undistracted by their lack of understanding, Jesus told the woman, "Thy faith hath saved thee, go in peace," without a single reference to her exact sins. All that seemed to matter was the quickest end to what was wrong so she could begin to live what is right.

We cannot grow by merely avoiding what is wrong. The things we think, feel, and act, which help us become better, must be actually lived. The bad thing about wrong is that it hurts our attempts to grow and wastes the time needed to practice and live what is right. Since we have only a certain amount of time on earth, those who spend more of it doing right will be more highly developed than those who waste time doing wrong. Exceptions to this are when learning something can be achieved in less time than a lifetime. Then, one who has done wrong can change and live right, fulfilling the same conditions as those who lived right all along. Generally speaking, however, those who love unselfishly for longer periods, for example, will be more highly developed than those who love briefly. The more time we spend doing right things, the greater will be our progress toward being like God.

No doubt this is one reason why the Savior's life focused on what helped people become better and did not emphasize possible punishments for wrongdoing. If someone had misbehaved, the Savior encouraged him to quickly start doing better in order to use the time most wisely. This is dramatically evident in the well-known conversation between Jesus and the woman caught in adultery (John 8). He dispersed her accusers by saying, "He that is without sin among you, let him first cast a stone at her." A moment later He asked, "Woman, where are those thine accusers? Hath no man condemned thee?" She said, "No man, Lord." And Jesus said, "Neither do I condemn thee: go, and sin no more." In other words, "Now go and do righteous works."

Modern Child Discipline

The authors of most books about child discipline make an assumption that leads many to miss what the Savior taught. They assume that when a child misbehaves, it is important for parents to apply a consequence. While these consequences might stop a child from misbehaving, there is no real guarantee children will begin to do what is better just because they have faced a consequence. There is little to be learned positively, for example, from being grounded, sent to a room, spanked, placed on a chair, or yelled at for doing wrong. Consequences are more effective if they are coupled with the additional events described later in this chapter.

Further, a punishment or consequential approach places the parent's behavior after the child's so that we are responding to what they do rather than leading them to do what is right. Our attention is often so misplaced that many parents fail to even think about what is right. The following example illustrates how many of us get caught up in reacting to what our children do. When teaching a parenting class, I was asked a question by one mother. "How do you stop a child from taking his toys apart and throwing the pieces around?" Notice that her question showed she was responding to what her child did. I replied by asking her how she wanted him to take care of his toys. I was surprised when the answer showed she did not listen to the question. "I can't stand it," she said. I had to ask her two more times until she finally heard my question. Then she responded with "I don't know." The solution to her problem of course was to create a program of toy care and teach that to her son. Instead, she was trying to stop misbehavior by spanking him, sitting him on a chair, and taking similar actions, only to find that a four-year-old was defeating her.

Understanding Children's Motives

The fact that Jesus responded so differently to each person who made requests to Him suggests that He was able to discern something unique about each one. His compassion for others was communicated to them by His efforts to see into their hearts and examine their intentions. He usually did this, rather than pass judgment about the obvious sin.

All parents need to correct the misbehavior of their children, and a consideration of the Savior's example shows a method that is not often found in books about child management. The focus is on motivating children to do what is right both by teaching them what right is and by using their misbehavior. The first part of this process is called understanding, because it requires parents to take the time to learn what motivates a child's actions rather than just to yell or angrily punish. There are some reasons why understanding is important. First, any wrong creates guilt or shame that creates a desire to be undetected. This alienates from other people the one who misbehaves. The wrongdoers judge themselves through the rejection they think others would show if they knew of the wrong that was done. "No one could love me," they think. "I am worthless," is the conclusion. Compassionate understanding of children's reasons or motives allows us to communicate that we recognize what they did as part of human life. They will feel better because they know we know. Taking the time to understand children's motives enables them to reenter the emotional tie with their parents.

Second, taking time to understand children's reasons improves parents' abilities to respond appropriately to the misbehavior. Our response to misbehavior needs to match the intentions of the child. To be truly just, we must understand before we react otherwise. Third, knowing the reasons why children misbehave will help us identify what must be done to help them do what is right. It will help us reach a solution of truly correcting the misbehavior. Fourth, the time we take to understand them (not agree or disagree with them) creates another important condition: our time and our compassion will make it more likely that children will come to us with their problems rather than hide them and risk making them worse. We can better share in the years of adjustment and changes of youth. We need to know what children were thinking about when they did what was wrong. If they are impulsive and have no intentions, we can teach them to make choices. Children may be unaware of their reasons and can be helped to increased awareness of them. If they had reasons they can identify, we must be able to correct their thinking as well as their actions.

Young children, for example, are usually not fully aware of the reasons for their actions. Because they may not be able to talk about them, it is useful for us to have some scheme we can use to understand them without depending on their ability to tell us.

Suppose, for example, a child comes in from playing outdoors and sits at the dinner table. During dinner he makes several strange noises and teases his sister by making snide remarks. His parents can simply respond to this and say something like, "Stop what you are doing or leave the table." Another alternative is to recognize that his actions have some underlying reason which can be discovered. While it is important to stop the inappropriate actions, his parents could do so in a way that takes into account what happened before dinner or what else might be motivating the child. If we suspend our judgment and response until we have hunted for and found this underlying reason, we will communicate without speaking that we care about our child and are attempting to match what we do with what the child feels. This attempt to understand is how we maintain emotional rapport. It also softens the child's feelings. Our indifference to the causes of children's behavior usually results in insecurity, increased separation between us, and resistance to change.

James Hymes wrote *Understanding Your Child* to describe the importance of parents' suspending their judgment and to help them observe and better understand children's motivations. He suggested there were four basic reasons or causes of children's actions. He gave some clues of how these causes could be identified and some suggestions on what parents could do. These can be seen in table 5.1.

Table 5.1
Understanding Children

Causes	Clues	Parental Responses
A Stage of Growth Children act in ways that fit their stage of development. These are caused by natural development. Example: learning to talk or wanting friends at about 3-4 years of age.	Every child acts in the same way at about the same time. Further, you acted the same way. Examples: 1. using strange words at about 14 years. 2. "hating" girls or boys. 3. "romance" at age 6-7.	Avoid doing much of anything. Children will grow out of it. Parental overreaction (unless the child is in danger) can prevent growth from taking place.
Unfulfilled Need Children have needs for belonging, security, control, and attention.	The child has an "electric" quality. Child will act the same way in most places. Emotions are very intense and stressful.	Adjust your behavior to improve emotional conditions for your child. Fill the emotional need.
Environment Cue Child responds to a cue somewhere in his environment (e.g., showing off when a neighbor visits).	Child acts a certain way only when the cue is present. Does not act the same way in all places.	Identify the cue and change it or help the child adapt to it more effectively.
Not Knowing How Some children act the way they do because they do not know how to do something.	Usually accompanied by crying, avoidance, complaining.	Take the time to teach the child how to successfully perform the task.

The ideas suggested in table 5.1 are especially useful for parents of young children who may not be able to tell of the reasons for misbehavior. As I have suggested, understanding the causes of children's behavior allows us to be more just in our response to them. Further, we can then be more effective in correcting misbehavior, because our actions will seem more reasonable to our children. As a result, children will come to know they can approach us when they have made mistakes instead of hiding them from us.

When children grow older they become more complex. As they acquire better language ability, they are more skilled at pretending and at hiding their misbehavior as well as their motivations from us. We can adjust to this by acquiring a new method of learning of their intentions. We need to keep in mind that it is as important for them to know their reasons for acting as it is for us to understand. Older children will often reveal their intentions through a discussion that is more a nonjudgmental inquiry and less a tense interrogation (although tense questioning sessions work well sometimes, too).

When older children are discovered at misbehaving, they are usually willing to explain their reasons in order to justify themselves. Remaining calm to create a climate for good discussion, we can ask, "Tell me what you were thinking when you did it." In the case of misbehavior, children will usually blame someone or something. If we argue or judge to point out their foolishness at first, they will stop talking and start feeling we are unfair. We need to clarify their thoughts by summarizing what was said. If a child has failed to do some task and explains that some friend kept him from doing it, his parents could say, "So you were not able to do this because of your friend." Having used this idea already, he'll agree. Having inquired and then summarized, the parents are in a great position to help correct a child's thoughts as well as the behavior. We need to remember, however, that taking the time to understand the child's reasons for misbehavior will first result in excuses and justification, which can be used to teach them if we avoid arguing or belittling them for the reasons they give. In the foregoing example, the parents listened and learned that their child believed a friend distracted him from doing a task. The parents summarized what the child said and the child agreed. Now the parents can say, "I want to know why your friend was more important to you than what I asked you to do." By learning the child's excuse, the parents can help the child correct his reasoning and realize his incorrect choice. Then the parents are still able to deal with the undone work.

Some parents complain about their children's inability to assume responsibility for their own actions as shown by the excuses their children give. It is tempting to immediately point out the inadequacy of the excuse or criticize the child for trying to place the blame on someone else. We cannot, however, "make" our children be responsible, but we can discuss with them their excuses and attempts to shift responsibility in order to help them reason in ways more acceptable to us and choose more responsible ways to act. It only requires some patient persistence in asking children if they think their reasons are "good ones" or if they do "feel they are partly responsible." This approach eventually will help children acknowledge their true intent.

Sometimes children are unwilling to talk about their reasons. We need not put direct pressure on them to do so except to ask, wait, ask again, and perhaps refuse desired privileges until they explain themselves. This works unless there is some immediate need to confront something. If we listen calmly, collect their reasons, and ask them why their reasons seemed better than doing what was correct, they will usually tell us and we can begin helping them evaluate their motives.

A frantic mother telephoned to ask if I would talk with her son: She and her daughter had been shopping when the little girl pointed to some beer and said, "That is what Scott was drinking the other night." When Scott came home from school, his mother cornered him and got him to admit he drank the beer. Then she tried to get him to promise never to do it again. Scott refused. She called his father, who came home early to join the fray. After an hour or so of the parents demanding and Scott refusing, the boy arose and left the house. Although he returned at midnight, his parents were concerned about his "running away" and his drinking.

When I met later with all three of them, the parents showed concern as I asked Scott to tell about the drinking episode. As he described drinking with some of his friends, I asked about his reasons. He said, "Everybody was drinking and I didn't want to feel stupid." At that point, the father began to preach something about "living your own standards," but I interrupted him so Scott could finish. I asked him how he liked beer. He said it didn't taste very good. "How much did you drink?" I asked. "Only part of a can," he replied, "then I poured the rest into the sink." His mother exclaimed, "Why didn't you tell us?" Scott's victorious reply was, "Because you never asked." Scott and his parents learned the importance of understanding the reasons for one's actions. Then we talked about whether Scott's reasons were the ones he really wanted to have if the same situation arose again. We concluded the discussion with what he might do and say differently.

We should not forget that children follow our example of the way we talk about ourselves. If we blame others for what we do then children will usually do the same. If we use reasons to excuse ourselves, children may learn that. It is also true, however, that thoughtful explanations of our reasons and intentions expressed to children help them learn to identify and explain their own.

There are times, of course, when a swift parental reaction to children is the best course of action. There are also times when no response is best. Most of the time when we inquire to find what children think are their reasons for acting a certain way, they will be more prepared to correct themselves. This process is more important than most of us have been taught. It allows us to teach children how to think as well as how to act. It enables us to match our discipline to what they do. Most important, it prepares them for the next part of the Savior's plan for correcting misbehavior.

Admission: Accepting Responsibility

On one occasion my wife and I hoped to teach our children more positive table manners by showing them as many negative things as possible. Instead of benefiting by this performance, our children applied the ironic law of childhood imitation. This law suggests that positive examples must be portrayed several times before they have enough value for children to imitate. An example of something we do not want our children to follow, like poor grammar or discourteous eating manners, only has to be observed once in order for children to imitate it. It took several days before we could rid our children of what we had inadvertently taught them.

This one experience taught us the importance of presenting to children a clear idea of what we thought was right for them to do. We have learned, of course, that the better we have taught and explained what is right, the easier it is for children to understand what is wrong. At the time, we did not know that we were preparing our children to participate in an important part of an effective plan to correct misbehavior.

Latter-day Saints are taught that true repentance is accompanied by confession. False repentance is an unsuccessful attempt to change. These attempts usually fail because the person attempting to change retains some notion that he or she did not fully choose to do wrong, that someone or something else is responsible. Confession is self-admission that the person did wrong and chose to do it. This admission is the prerequisite of authentic change.

Without realizing it, a blamer who attempts to shift responsibility through his accusations is expressing no faith in himself. Whoever or whatever "made" him do wrong is, in his mind, made more powerful than the blamer. Admission of responsibility is a statement of faith in the person who admits it because the person acknowledges that his actions result from his choices. Misbehavior can be better corrected after an admission of this type because the individual believes and feels he is in more control of himself.

When the Savior brought about change in people's lives, He asked them to acknowledge or admit their faith in the Savior and in themselves. Jesus had to help Peter grow from a person with limited dedication and consistency to one of devotion and discipleship. Even though Peter proclaimed belief in Christ on more than one occasion, he was at first sometimes weak in his testimony. During the evening of the Savior's stay in the Garden of Gethsemene, Peter, along with James and John, were taken to an inner gate and asked by the Savior to "tarry ye here, and watch with me" (Matthew 26:38). When the Savior returned, he found them asleep and awakened them. This occurred three times. Later, when Peter was accused of being a follower of Christ, he fearfully denied knowing Jesus. He did it three times and sorrowed thereafter.

After Peter had gone to the Sea of Galilee, the resurrected Savior visited him. Peter leapt from his boat to reach the shore quickly. Later, during their meal, the Savior turned and asked Peter, "Lovest thou me more than these [the things to eat]?" The Savior asked him to admit his faith. One can imagine Peter's chagrin when he was asked to admit his devotion three times. There is no record after this of any faltering on Peter's part.

Children are more likely to correct misbehavior when they sense and admit the extent of their choice in doing it. It is possible to ask, "Did you choose to do this?" or "How much responsibility do you feel for what has been done?" These and other questions like them lead children to examine themselves, confront their actions, and understand their responsibility in the matter.

The discussion about admission should continue until children openly admit their choice in the matter. If they will not do so, parents can leave, saying, "We'll talk again." Children who think they have escaped will later ask for privileges. None should be granted, in my opinion, until a further discussion takes place. Sometimes several days pass until a child has thought through the question, has faced himself with the answer, and has developed the courage to admit it. Parents can even acknowledge how difficult the task is and warmly encourage a child's efforts. If we are calm, warm, and persistent, the child will eventually say, "I did it. I made the choice." This admission states the return of faith in the child, who is more ready to begin the change.

Consequences

To growing and developing children, learning about what we, their parents, think to be good, what we think to be true, and what we think to be right will help them make fewer mistakes and give direction to their growth. Before we consider using consequences for misbehavior, we need to set in motion an active teaching plan in which children are exposed to the good, true, and right. This alone will reduce the incidents of misbehavior and increase their opportunities for succeeding with their parents. When the times of misbehavior do come, however, we want them to have a clear distinction between the misbehavior and what is right so they will assuredly know they have done wrong. Otherwise they may mistakenly think, as many do, that something wrong is not that bad and continue doing it.

Actively teaching what we want our children to do also lets us take the initiative and increases our influence. If we just react in attempts to stop misbehavior, we will feel increasingly frustrated and helpless. Parents do not usually act their best in this circumstance. We deserve to be more calm than hurried, more patient than angry. We help ourselves by taking the time to show and to tell our children what we truly want them to do that is right as we see it.

There might be occasions when a specific punishment is useful in helping children stop doing what is wrong and begin doing right. We have even heard the suggestion that a consequence is effective if it is natural instead of being imposed by parents who want to dramatize the wrong and motivate children to improve. This means that the misbehavior prevents a child from getting something or doing something else. An example of this is preventing a child from eating because he or she has been late. It is natural because the child's "lateness" has prevented him from eating at the regular time.

Usually, after understanding a child's reasons and bringing a child to an admission of what he has done, the best consequence is to rectify the wrong and require children to do what would have been right. On one occasion, I found that two of my children had been quarreling instead of talking things out and cooperating. After asking them how much they each had contributed and obtaining a weak statement of responsibility, I explained they would have to "practice" doing right what they had showed they could not do. "What if we don't do it?" one asked. I replied, "You won't eat or watch TV until you do." That fact sank in. "What do we have to do?" the other asked. "Well," I replied, "I am going to have you plant a few flowers together so you will have to cooperate. I want you to talk about how you will do it before you start. Then, when you are finished, I want you to play a game together without arguing." Realizing the consequence was less severe than they expected, both participated. They learned to do right what they had not done earlier. The best use of wrong actions is as a means to teach children to learn what is right. Some examples are shown in table 5.2.

This works well with older children, too. If children are late coming home, for example, we can ask the next day about their reasons and encourage them to tell what they chose to do instead of coming home. The consequence is to try again and get it right. This is much more effective than an argument or a punishment when children do not admit their responsibility and resent us as a result. Suppose an older child undressed some younger neighbor children to inspect their bodies. What he did not do was care about and show respect for others. Understanding his reasons, listening to his admission of the choices he made can be followed by requesting that he learn about sexual knowledge and show ways to care for and respect other people. This consequence clearly distinguishes between what is wrong and what is right.

I suggested to one set of parents that they have their son, who showed a lack of care for someone, volunteer for work in a pediatric unit at the local hospital. There he read stories to children who were ill and became acquainted with the importance of being considerate to others.

Five boys (ages nine to eleven) sneaked behind a house and rolled up newspaper to smoke. They were caught and asked to line up for a discussion. "What were your reasons?" each was asked.

Table 5.2
Misbehavior and Consequences

Typical Misbehavior	(a)What Children Could Not Do and (b) What They Can Do to Practice
1. Quarreling about a toy	(a) Calmly talk over differences and learn to share. (b) Use a game or a joint task.
2. Quarreling about one's mistreatment of the other	(a) Show respect and consideration for others. (b) Rehearse caring for the needs of someone else.
3. Hitting in anger	(a) Control anger and show care for someone else. (b) Care for a pet or a plant in order to make it live.
4. Lying by misrepresenting the facts of a situation	(a) Feel confident enough to say what is correct. (b) Ask children to tell what they see, what people said, and other details of several situations.
5. Failing to keep promises	(a) Feel responsible enough to keep their word. (b) Ask children to make promises about several things and encourage them to keep them.
6. Not coming home on time	(a) Regulate their activities to be responsible to family rules. (b) Buy an inexpensive watch or loan them one so they can go out and come back in 10 minutes, then in 20 minutes, then in 30 minutes, and so forth.
7. Doing work poorly and hiding it	(a) Have a sense of doing something well. (b) Give them a small task and ask that they repeat it until it is done well.
8. Mistreating a friend	(a) Responsibly handle social situations. (b) Require that they thoroughly explain the incident, their feelings about it, then develop and carry out a plan to create a positive social experience for someone.

Then, after hearing the answer, I asked each boy, "Did you do it?" Knowing they had been seen, some nodded assent and others murmured a subdued "yes." "Was there anyone who said, 'No, this is wrong and I won't do it'?" They all agreed that Craig had refused. Since Craig was not there, we found him and had him tell us his reasons and admit his choices. "Wow, that's great," I said. "I am going to tell your parents." And I did. This was a lesson to the other boys of what is right and the rewards that right actions bring.

Of course, there are children who are so distant from us and out of control they will neither stop wrong nor rehearse right. For those children, external control is necessary, through any reasonable means. For those who are in the bond of affection, the steps of understanding, obtaining an admission of one's choices, and practicing the right, work effectively.

There are, of course, two consequences for any wrong act. One is the effect on the person who misbehaves. This happens differently for each person depending on what is done and why. The other consequence is the learning that is necessary to prevent the misbehavior from happening again. When we ask children to rehearse what is right after they have done wrong, we help them feel that we know that they know inside how to do what is right. The basis for a life of righteousness is knowing what is the right thing to do and doing it with the intention of fulfilling our own expectations and responding to the encouragement of those who know we have a knowledge of truth.

6   Virtue

Helping our children know God requires that we teach an understanding of Him. He possesses many godly characteristics, of course, but there is one so important that it is revealed many times and in many ways. This is the characteristic of exactness and stability which we call virtue. Regardless of temptation or other influences, God and His Son Jesus Christ regulate themselves and are divine.

If we desire to help our children internalize God's laws, we must teach them to be virtuous. It is not a simple task. For one thing, it is a lifelong task. For another, virtue is learned by a complex set of conditions. It is difficult because parental examples of virtue must also be shown. Our task is made easier though by understanding the Savior's teachings. Through the gospel, we can learn how to teach virtue to our children.

One day early in His ministry, Jesus walked to a hill followed by a multitude of people from Decapolis, Galilee, Jerusalem, Judea, and beyond Jordan. He had been in Galilee preaching, and His fame had been widely spread. He stood silently watching as the people followed and then settled themselves. After their voices were quieted He began to speak. What He taught was unfamiliar. One after another He gave suggestions to them for situations in their relationships with others and with God. He suggested as He first gave the beatitudes that our feelings about ourselves need to be positive. He described how believers in God should be loyal and set an example for others.

In the Sermon on the Mount the Savior sought to encourage people to treat spiritual things with increased importance. The Ten Commandments, for example, taught people not to kill, but He now said that anger without cause was also wrong. Following this He introduced an idea which has great significance for the quality of life we are able to give our children. He proposed that the true and best way to live as mortals is to have an inner sense of control or agency and not allow other people or situations to determine what one does or how one acts.

He did not state this idea in the specific words of our day, but introduced it through several examples. He said we should turn the other cheek; and this would not let the other person control our actions. If someone sues us for a coat, we should show our self-control by giving our cloak also. If someone takes our freedom away by forcing us to go one mile, we can walk a second mile with that person in order to restore the dignity of our own control. After teaching these ideas, the Savior indicated that our sense of self-control needs to develop to the mature level of loving our enemies, blessing those who curse us, doing good to those who hate us, and praying for those who persecute and despitefully use us.

This ability to control ourselves is improved if we try to avoid public honor and seek to do good in secret. Further, He admonished us to focus more on the events of today and worry less about the future, to not run faster than we are able and not concern ourselves about things which we cannot change. By following His teachings and doing this, we can keep ourselves calm and not give in to the harmful effects of stress.

I believe the real purpose for all these suggestions was to help us pay attention to the whispering voices within instead of getting caught up in the pressures of external happenings. This is the way virtue is learned, by controlling ourselves and reflecting on the voice of conscience, the Spirit of truth, before we act.

This idea also suggests that people too influenced by the pressures of the world will lose their sense of control over themselves and because of the loss, possess less virtue. For this reason, I believe, we are told: "Let virtue garnish thy thoughts unceasingly; then shall thy confidence wax strong in the presence of God; and the doctrine of the priesthood shall distil upon thy soul as the dews from heaven. The Holy Ghost shall be thy constant companion." (D&C 121:45-46.)

Virtue is the ability to regulate our thoughts, emotions, and actions. This self-mastery and the power that comes from it is learned gradually. As children acquire it, they can better resist temptation, delay impulsive acts, regulate their moods, and concentrate without being distracted. Later, virtue is the power to avoid succumbing to peer pressure in order to maintain one's values. It is the ability to control sexual urges and to live law-abiding, honorable lives.

Children come into life with little thought except to feel comfortable through others providing love, food, and dry clothes. Children's next tasks are to learn physical skills and to speak. Their social life with friends begins at about three years of age. An observant parent could see that children of this age believe that everyone thinks as they think. They show little awareness that they are separate individuals with their own thoughts and unique feelings. This condition prevents them from feeling responsible for their actions. "Someone or something else" causes their problems and is to blame for mistakes and makes them unhappy. When parents find a mistake, for example, and ask, "Who did this?" children are quite sure it was someone other than themselves.

As they mature, however, children gradually discover that other people may think differently than they do and become more aware of themselves as individuals separate from others. Once parents understand this idea, they can watch children begin to reflect about their own ideas and feelings. Children need to show a recognition or awareness of how they act as well as what other people do. This introspection gives knowledge about themselves, which is the basis of virtue or self-control. Unaware at first of the true lifelong task ahead to learn virtue, children four to five years of age already have begun the process of acquiring the ability to regulate themselves.

Virtue Is Spiritual Growth

Some parts of virtue are learned by the way parents treat their children. Most of virtue, when it is learned well, stems from what a parent actually is. Children appear to be exactly as virtuous as their parents. This does not mean that the specific inappropriate actions of parents will always be copied by their children. It does mean that parents are able to regulate themselves, and that in a variety of aspects their children tend to live in a similar way. There is a scriptural story, however, showing the effects of parental example on children.

For many years, David, the king of Israel, was a fine, noble, and virtuous man. When he became king his people grew and prospered. He was given additional wives by the Lord, but on one occasion as he was on the roof of his palace at night, he watched Bathsheba washing herself. At his request she came and lay with him. She conceived. She informed him of her circumstance, and David reacted by having her husband, Uriah, sent home from the battlefield, expecting that he would go home to his wife. But Uriah would not do this while his comrades in arms were roughing it at the front. After a few days, David sent Uriah back to the war with a note to Joab, the leader of David's army. The note ordered that Uriah be placed in the forefront of the hottest battle and other troops withdrawn from him so he would be killed. This was accomplished and David took Bathsheba to wife, an event sown in a legacy of adultery and murder.

A few years later one of David's sons, Amnon, became "vexed" with his half-sister Tamar. By deceit he lured her into his home and grabbed her insisting that she lie with him. "Nay, my brother," she replied, "do not force me; for no such thing ought to be done in Israel; do not thou this folly" (2 Samuel 13:12). Her protests were in vain. Amnon forced himself upon her and then became angry at himself and at her, sending her away. She went to the home of her full brother. Absalom, a favorite of King David, was angry at Amnon. After a few months he organized a hunting trip conspiring to kill Amnon, which was accomplished. He fled but was found. In the next few years he secretly organized a conspiracy to overthrow his father. War broke out, a tense struggle ensued. During one battle, Joab found Absalom who had fled and was caught by his head in a tree. Joab killed him. David's legacy of lack of control was visited upon his children. In this case, the sins of the sons were the same as their father's.

This example illustrates that in the case of virtue, many children become like their parents. But many virtuous parents do not have virtuous children, for example, so there must be more to it than parental example. We can examine the spiritual way children learn virtue.

I am using the term *spiritual growth* as Nephi did who wrote that when a man speaks by the power of the Holy Ghost, the power of the Holy Ghost carries it into the hearts of the children of men (2

Nephi 33:1). This scripture suggests that parents can, through spiritual means, transmit something to children without necessarily having to speak it. Through many of these spiritual communications, children recognize that virtue is most necessary if they are to live a happy life. The conditions we present to our children in order to accomplish this are familiar to most Latter-day Saints. One is a testimony borne by faithful parents. Another is gospel knowledge taught by caring parents. Another is a sense of freedom or free agency that parents give by asking children to consider alternatives and then choose. This must be done without parental dominance, overprotectiveness, or indulgence.

In regard to freedom, one set of parents were having difficulty getting a son to do his homework. When he procrastinated they reminded him, but then they grew impatient. If one or both parents became angry enough he started his work, but usually he was not enthusiastic. After repeating this sequence on many occasions, they finally decided to make their son choose for himself. Their conversation was similar to the following:

Parents: What are you going to do about your homework?

Son: I don't know.

Parents: Well, it's your choice. You have to decide yourself.

Son: Really?

Parents: Let's take a look at what your choice really is. What will you feel like if you do your homework? And what will happen at school tomorrow?

Son: I'll get a higher grade, and I will feel better.

Parents: What will happen if you don't do it?

Son: I won't get a good grade.

Parents: That's right. But what about you? What kind of person will you be?

Son: What do you mean?

Parents: Well, if you can't do something a bit difficult in order to make yourself a success, what kind of person are you?

Son: Lazy, I guess.

Parents: Do you want to be like that?

Son: No.

Parents: What are you going to do about homework tonight?

Son: I don't want to do it.
Parents: I'll help you if you decide to do it.

Their method was not an instant solution. But they continued each time he balked, and he began to show more initiative. They couldn't tell whether it was due to the freedom he felt or to avoid the long conversation about choosing. In any case, he improved.

Freedom through choices communicates an unspoken spiritual message that one is responsible for himself. When children are taught how to decide and are expected to think through the advantages and disadvantages of alternatives, they also learn to feel stronger and more in control of themselves.

Another condition which spiritually communicates the importance of virtue is that of consequences children choose for their own actions. If children agree to some consequence before they do something or through discussion with parents afterward, then they will more likely accept the consequences and learn self-control from it. If parents simply impose a consequence to punish, children will learn less and may resent their parents more.

In addition to freedom and chosen consequences, virtue is learned by children whose parents exercise the "paradox of authority." This paradox suggests that parents should feel and have a great deal of authority over their children, but actually use it infrequently. Parents who impose excessive amounts of authority often find they remove a vital sense of virtue from children. Even if compliance to our rules is achieved, children do not learn virtue. Conformity is a response to someone else's authority, while obedience, the true form of virtue, requires that children exercise some sense of their own agency. Children will not choose to obey nor will they learn virtue if they are merely responding out of fear from parents' harshness. Children of abusive parents often have difficulty being virtuous.

The inconsistency of our response to children often prevents them from having a virtuous attitude. Virtue is not gained when we organize rules and fail to consistently enforce them. Virtue is not learned when we tell children what they should do but then show them a contradictory example. Virtue is not valued when we show a lack of caring by using manipulative rewards to entice them. Virtue becomes a part of children's lives the more we regularly emphasize and exemplify what we value.

Children's Emotional Style

Our efforts to teach virtue depend a great deal on the nature of our children. Every parent knows that children can be very different from each other. Sometimes the differences are surprisingly great, especially when we think that our own children should be somewhat alike. The uniqueness of each child suggests that we need to understand each differently than others and that we need to be able to adapt our parenting to each child in order for us to be the best teachers of virtue.

Of the many ways to understand children, the one used most often by parents is a child's emotional style. Children inherit certain emotional characteristics that can be observed shortly after birth. Some children continue these traits throughout their life while other traits are influenced and changed by children's experiences in home and society. If we are sincerely interested in helping our children learn the self-control we call virtue, then we can learn to use their emotional style as a basis for how we teach them.

Behavioral scientists have developed many labels to describe children's emotional styles. Of these, there are two dimensions that seem to be the best way to understand children's emotions: intensity and security. Children's emotions are said to be high or low in each of these. The characteristics these labels describe are shown in table 6.1.

There is evidence that children's emotional styles determine how easy or difficult it is for them to learn self-control. The amount of security they feel and the degree of intensity they display can help parents organize their efforts.

Virtue and Security

There are many stories about successful adults who as children had cheerful dispositions. They seem to have been favored children right from the start. Of course, it is not that these children inherit success. Rather, some children appear to have inherited a sense of assurance or security about themselves and happily live with parents who nurture it. As it turns out, children who are more insecure and inhibited can, with parental help, also be just as successful in developing self-control.

Table 6.1
Children's Emotional Styles

Emotional Dimension	Children's Behavior
High Intensity	Children's emotions are expressed with intensity. Whether positive or negative emotions, they are displayed in ways obvious to others.
Low Intensity	Children display positive and negative emotions in an inhibited way showing mild reactions and passive responses.
High Security	Children are confident, uninhibited, cheerful, socially aggressive, calm, and attentive.
Low Security	Children are anxious, difficult to comfort, and lack responsiveness. They are distractable and fearful in social situations.

Many researchers have studied children's sense of security and their self-control or resistance to temptation. In these studies it is clear that the cheerfulness and attentiveness of secure children enable them to control themselves better than children who are unhappy, insecure, non-attentive. In one study, children who listened to happy family sounds (e.g., "I love you" or singing) were able to work on a task longer and were less impulsive than children who had listened to unhappy sounds (e.g., a child crying or an angry parent). This example and others like it show that when children feel assurance they are better able to regulate themselves.

We do not know how much security children learn or how much they inherit. We do know that when parents themselves are cheerful, are confident, and are calmer as compared to excited, their children have a greater sense of assurance. When parents are angry, insecure, and impatient, children are also more insecure and more susceptible to impulsive actions.

Several years ago I read a short story about a little boy whose parents noticed he spent a lot of time playing at his friend's home. Usually when he came home he was cheerful, but after a few minutes, grew silent and less responsive. After this had taken place several times, his mother asked him why he enjoyed going to his friend's home. "Oh, Mother," he responded, "they sing over there." Curious, the mother visited her neighbor and told of her son's statement. Somewhat embarrassed, the woman described a family emotional climate filled with songs, affection, and happy sounds. The boy's mother now understood her son's actions and resolved to make her family a singing family.

I learned firsthand about the influence parents have on their children's sense of assurance when my oldest daughter was seven years old. My wife mentioned one morning that my daughter had had an unhappy experience the previous day and suggested that I talk to her about it. I went to her room and found her happily brushing her hair in front of the mirror. "Hi, Dad," she brightly greeted as she saw me at the door. "Hi, yourself," I replied and went in and sat on her bed. "Mother tells me you had a very sad experience yesterday," I began in the sympathetic sad tones I thought she would appreciate. "What?" she answered in reply, not connecting my question to the experience already forgotten. "Would you like to tell me about it?" I persisted. I thought afterward she must have wondered what I was talking about, because at this time she was completely happy and content. Finally, she remembered her sad experience, came over to the bed, and sat beside me. "Oh, yeah," she said in a subdued tone and began to tell me what happened to a friend at school. The change from happiness to sadness was so abrupt one could not have missed it. It was then I realized I had created her sadness by my expectation that she was sad. As she continued to tell of this experience, she began to feel so unhappy she cried. I saw the need to encourage her and say comforting, positive words. It took only a few moments for her to change back to the cheerfulness I first saw as I entered her room. I learned from this that if I were to have cheerful children I would need to be that way, too.

All children are not as open to a parent's influence as this child was to mine. But, over time, the degree of secure assurance a child feels is usually given or removed by their parents and family life. Since our children may differ in the degree of security they feel, most parents will have some secure children and others who are less secure. Correctly adapting to each child helps parents be more effective in teaching.

Virtue and Emotional Intensity

Emotionally intense children usually are characterized by explosive episodes of anger, impulsiveness, teasing, sudden mood changes, and opposition to parents' rules and requests. Children with low emotional intensity, at the other extreme, are often passive, somewhat detached from others, and can be overly sensitive to how they are treated. They may also be dependent on others and take extreme measures to seek protectiveness. Children who have moderate amounts of intensity are easier for parents to understand and usually enable parents to feel more successful. They are, according to research findings, more likely to develop a strong sense of self-control than children at either extreme (e.g., very intense or very passive).

When one intense child was prevented from doing something he wanted, he showed his emotional intensity by tantrums. He opposed his parents' announcement that it was time for him to "go to bed" and would argue or disagree frequently. He showed early signs of good athletic ability but was very competitive and was excessively discouraged if his team lost.

As he grew older he demonstrated impulsiveness in many ways. One was by taking things that didn't belong to him. After these times he could not recall his reasons for stealing. He often responded without thinking to what his friends wanted and gave little regard to family rules about time to be home or restrictions about when he could play. His parents had tried all they knew and felt like failures. Their attitudes about him were less positive than about their other children although they had a hard time admitting it to themselves. He often told lies to hide the results of his impulsive acts. During his teenage years he frequently violated curfews and experimented with shoplifting, drugs, and alcohol. He was finally picked up by the juvenile authorities, and through their supervision received psychological help which involved his parents. After a long time, he learned to regulate himself better and more constructively.

Jenny was ten years old when I first met her. She appeared extremely passive, even lethargic as she sat on the couch. When asked to speak, she looked downward and often did not answer except for a yes or no. Her school teacher thought her to be shy and tried several techniques to bring her into more social contact. At home she spent quite a bit of time alone in her room listening to music, reading, or just sitting. She had had only one friend at a time and played irregularly with her.

It was possible to see that she had some more intense feelings because her mouth twitched, her face and neck flushed occasionally, and the muscles of her body would sometimes tighten and sometimes relax. Few of her emotions were displayed through her voice tones or by more expressive physical actions. She clearly inhibited the expression of her feelings for some reason. This low intensity was shown in school work, in family life, and in social situations. For her, learning virtue would require a different approach from parents than for the extra-intense child.

Because of their adaptability, moderately intense children are more likely to be self-regulating than children who are very intense or very passive. This may seem to contradict the idea that a person with virtue will hold to ideals and values consistently regardless of the situation. We can understand, however, that moderately intense children are more aware of their own emotions. Children with extremely high or low intensity are more aware of what is external to them. The consistency of virtue comes from being aware of and controlling our desires in many different situations. When children are focused too much on what others think or when they attend to other things, they are more likely to be erratic and influenced by something other than their own ideals.

As we consider what parents might do for children who live with high or low intensity, notice that the emphasis is on helping them identify their own thoughts and feelings. The reason for this is that children who are either extremely high or extremely low in emotional intensity tend to direct their attention to external things. Their impulsiveness or passiveness can be improved by helping them develop strategies of action formed by knowing their thoughts and emotions.

Intensity and Security

When the degree of security is combined with a child's level of intensity, four emotional styles emerge. These are described in table 6.2. Also, I have provided some suggested parental skills for each type. I have included such general skills as expressing affection or creating lengthy conversations except where it is not useful to do so. I do not intend that the ideas presented be thought of as all that is necessary. I hope that I convey the idea that we need to adapt to each child to best help him learn self-control and virtue.

Table 6.2
Four Emotional Styles with Parental Strategies

Children's Emotional Style	How Children Act	What Parents Can Do
Secure High Intensity	1. Socially aggressive 2. Shows leadership among friends 3. Makes social mistakes like talking too much or saying inappropriate things 4. Adventurous 5. Challenges authority—often asks "why" or for reasons 6. Reacts quickly but calms quickly, too 7. Can talk openly with parents 8. Has fluctuating moods, but usually cheerful	A. Show examples of and require children to calmly talk about their emotional reactions B. Require child to develop a strategy for what he/she wants to accomplish C. Show high levels of affection which increases emotional control D. Require them to make choices about how they "will" act in a situation and hold them to their choice E. Refer them to their emotions when they are talking about themselves F. Use positive reinforcement strategies to improve responses G. Help them be aware of how to act in many different social situations H. Actively teach ways to control their emotions (i.e., talking about them, expecting control as a disciplinary measure, cooling off in a bedroom, etc.)
Secure Low Intensity	1. Mild fluctuations of mood 2. Generally cheerful and pleasant 3. Sometimes very passive and unresponsive 4. Will play tricks or perform secret acts of deceit 5. Occasionally says what people want to hear to remove pressure on themselves 6. Avoids confrontations but carries emotions for longer periods (e.g., grudge) 7. Usually performs tasks well	A. Expose them to social opportunities B. Teach strategies of emotional control (see H above) C. Use an emotion word vocabulary and engage them in many conversations D. Ensure they feel affection and attention (it is easy to ignore this child if they do well) E. Routine discipline systems of rules and consequences works well with these children

Insecure High Intensity	1. Emotionally explosive (e.g., tantrums) 2. Impulsively responds to external stimulus 3. Talks excessively 4. Tells lies to avoid responsibility 5. Fails to follow through on tasks 6. Opposition reaction when told what to do 7. Argues when told "no" 8. Adopts excitement shown by others 9. Expresses anger more when tired or hungry	A. Emphasize their need to control emotions and to have *strategies* of how they will act in specific situations, to *delay action* while they think (e.g., "stop, look, listen"), to have *vigilance* at watching for how people act and cues of social situations B. Use structured positive reinforcement techniques to control behavior C. Calm children before talking to them or correcting them D. Ignore tantrums E. Teach and rehearse how to act in situations they face (grocery store, church, school, etc.)
Insecure Low Intensity	1. Socially inhibited (isolates self) 2. Shows fear in many situations (e.g., shyness, blushing) 3. May have long periods of depression 4. Avoids challenges, fears new situations 5. Has difficulty talking to others	A. Involve them with groups of children and reinforce how well they get along B. Work to create conversations (and it can be work) C. Use pantomime or charades to teach emotions D. Help them develop a talent that can be used socially E. Use praise abundantly

Virtue and Adolescents

As our children grow older they naturally begin to learn to act appropriately in many situations. Learning to regulate themselves is, therefore, applied to those at that stage of life. For teenagers, this may mean self-control is learned for diet control, exercise, social situations with same-gender friends, dating experiences, study habits, doing chores at home, class behavior in school and church, sports events, and many family events.

As adults we have been through each of these and are more or less able to regulate ourselves in them. For many these situations and others present lifelong challenges. In any event, there is much we can do to help our children develop an increased sense of control over themselves. Most recognize that preliminary to any self-control is a feeling or attitude of responsibility for one's actions. When children first move into social situations, for instance, it is quite easy for them to feel that the responsibility for their actions belongs to someone who shares the situation with them. One of my children was explaining why he received a low grade from the eighth grade math teacher. Since his other grades were quite good, he seemed to feel justified in saying that the teacher was a poor teacher, she did not like him, and there was nothing he could do to get any higher grades. I listened quietly as he fleshed out his explanation with tidbits of information. After he was finished, I asked him, "Who has the grade on his report card, you or the teacher?" He said, "I do." "Then," I told him, "there is only one question: are you going to do what is necessary to improve it or let your feelings about this teacher get in the way?" "But," he sputtered, "she doesn't like me." "I know it is hard when you think the teacher doesn't like you, but what are you going to do?" He responded by improving his grade a little and then arranging to take math from a different teacher the following year. Both responses could be thought of as responsible considering his level of maturity.

There are many ways to communicate that each individual, not someone else, is responsible for what he or she does. In my experience this emphasis needs to be given often and firmly. The point of it is found when an individual is with others or faced with something enticing. It is easy for children to think that their actions are caused by other people or that the temptation is too great unless they possess a clear understanding that how they act is mostly a result of their decisions and less the influence of anyone or anything external.

Once personal responsibility is an accepted idea, the next step is to discuss specific situations and identify the appropriate thing to do in order to regulate themselves in each case. For example, children can be given a stopping technique and a distraction for a difficult circumstance. A girl confessed to consistently buying candy bars which she saw near the checkout register at a grocery store. Although she had tried to quit doing it, each time she was there she bought candy and ate it. She quit when she spent a few minutes each day imagining stop signs around the candy stand and visualized herself walking by without eating the candy. She also agreed to count the number of tiles, lights, and clocks from the candy stand to the end of the checkout counter. This worked because she had a stopping technique and used a distraction.

These same two conditions can be applied in different ways to any situation in which children may have a bit of difficulty regulating themselves. They can be used for a romance that gets out of control, or for invitations to drink or use other substances. One boy told of repeated attempts by friends to get him to drink beer. He told them no several times, but they did not stop asking until he said, "Listen, guys, I have made a deal with my dad, and I am not going to break it." Interestingly, his dad did not know about the "deal."

Another self-control device we can teach children is to overcome their fear of maintaining their standards. Children could be helped by thinking about the following ideas. It is true that mature people respect those with self-control, as do many youth. It is also true that many youth will be rejected or ridiculed if they do not go along with the requests of their friends. Just how bad is that type of rejection? How long does it last? What can a person do about it if it happens? Discuss these questions with children and help them think about what they will do. We can also tell them of personal experiences or those of other people who have stood for a correct principle when others would not. Such accounts tell our children if there is only one who will do what must be done, it can be one of them.

7 To Be and To Do

Children are well acquainted with the idea that they are growing, changing, and developing. Pictures of them are taken; relatives exclaim surprise at their growth since their last meeting. In America, schools have grade levels which mark age and maturity. Then, combined with home influences, children look forward to privileges based on their age. Any parent knows how children anticipate increased allowance, staying up longer, a driver's license, or a first date.

In addition to all of these, there are usually numerous informal ways parents signal acceptance of children's new maturity. These may include participation in important family decisions, going places with older children instead of having to stay with the younger, inclusion in more adult conversations where they hear adult ideas. From the children's viewpoint, another informal and important sign that parents recognize their children's maturity is signaled when the parents grant increased freedom.

All these family events symbolize the growth that is part of life. Added to new-found abilities discovered in their bodies, their minds, and their emotions, children are naturally led to think of the future and what it may bring. They think of the future so much more than they think of anything else. It is easy to understand then why they are so susceptible to parental influence. To children, parents are viewed as having walked ahead on the pathway of life and knowing what the future will bring for them. When parents, if they are at all credible, make statements about life and how to prepare for it, children do not casually listen. These statements are like instructions or recipes to be heard and followed.

One Sunday as I called my children to our family devotional, one teenage son complained about having to particpate because he "already got so much" in church and seminary. "Why do we have to do this?" he challenged. He was the type of thoughtful boy who would not accept a platitude or my authority as the reason. For a moment I was unfocused and I thought of "the Lord wants us to," or "the prophet has asked us to" and knew neither would satisfy him. "Suppose," I began, "I was fifty yards ahead of you on the pathway of life and it was my job to yell back and tell you what kind of shoes to wear. If you could not see me as you walked barefoot in soft, warm sand, what would you do if you heard me say to put on heavy shoes?" My son replied, "That depends on whether I trusted you." "Well," I answered, "I am yelling back to you that someday knowing about the scriptures will be among the most important knowledge you have."

That satisfied him I suppose, because he never raised the question again. As I have thought about that incident, I realized my answer seemed reasonable because it communicated to his soul's knowledge that he was still developing and one day might find that what I said was true.

Parents acquire tremendous influence from children's belief that we can tell and show them what they are developing into and what they must do to achieve their goals. To be fully responsible to our children, we must examine what they must do and how they must act in order for them to be a success, for whatever they understand our standards to be, both formally as we openly teach them and informally as they watch us, they will develop toward those standards. It is our parental prerogative to be more influential in our children's lives than anyone else can be. It is our parental obligation to learn how to help our children develop toward a standard of success that includes eternal life. It is our parental downfall if we inadequately teach our children and they reject our teachings, or if we fail to use this natural condition to help them and us. We must carefully examine what we believe a successful child is. Our children will discover what they think we value and grow toward it as surely as growing plants turn to any source of light.

The Character of Christ and the Character of Culture

Living in a world offering many versions of success, most Christians declare a desire to become like Christ but also face the need to make their way safely and successfully in society. As we examine the standards of success we place before our children, we need to consider both what the Savior taught and the influence of our culture on us. These two sources of information will give us an idea of what we are teaching our children to become.

Charles Jefferson wrote *The Character of Jesus* to emphasize the need to focus on Christ's personal attributes. He illustrated this need by suggesting that the New Testament writers were not interested in trifles.

> They cared nothing for his stature, the clothes he wore or the houses he lived in. He had none of the things which biographers are wont to expiate upon to the extent of many chapters. . . . His friends were all obscure. He was born in a stable, worked in a carpenter shop, taught for three years, and then died on a cross. . . . Everything is minimized and subordinated to that which is central and all important, the texture of his spirit and the attitude of his personality. With òne accord they cry "Behold the Man!" (Charles Jefferson, *The Character of Jesus* [Thomas Y. Crowelk & Co., 1908; reprinted, Salt Lake City: Parliament Publishers, 1968], p. 22.)

This author rightly suggested that followers of Christ need be concerned mostly with traits of character such as charity, forgiveness, honesty, love, courage, dependability, sincerity, and kindness. These, of course, are only a few examples. The point for us to recognize, however, is that they are qualities of the soul which are usually displayed in one's relationship to others. When positive, they are the parts of us which add up to *being* good or *being* righteous. They are the focus of what we are *to be* and what we want our children *to be* according to the gospel of Christ.

A significant part of this standard of success could be these qualities. Our example and teaching should focus on helping our children learn and live them. We only need to recognize that some special parental skills might be required in order for us to be effective. A sizeable portion of what we do as parents will be directed to these qualities; we will either help our children acquire them, ignore them, or learn something else.

As we live among our fellow beings, we form a society bond on language and common interests. Each society forms ways of transmitting its values to each coming generation. A culture consists of the values, beliefs, and practices we hold in common. For example, in America there is great emphasis on the value of productivity and acquiring possessions or estates. We also notice that emphasis is placed on holding prominent positions acquiring great power. These can be alluring to us for they are the cultural signs of success. This is confirmed in that we usually find that wealthy people do seem to have advantages over the poor as they have more opportunities to travel, to vacation, to obtain an education, and to acquire prominence. When parents of this culture love their children and want the best for them, they feel impelled to prepare them to achieve these advantages. In fact, our entire society may be thought of as organized around the means of acquiring these things. We transmit to our children through schools, churches, and families to value productivity, to obtain wealth, power, or prominence, and to plan their lives to obtain as much as possible of them. There are certainly many variations of this idea of success. Generally speaking, however, productivity is the chief goal of American society. In Latter-day Saint ideology, productivity is valued if it leads to self-sufficiency and quality family life. We are to be workers, but not as much to acquire possessions as to care for ourselves and contribute to others.

Our sense of urgency to organize is intensified when we encounter people who did not plan and do not succeed. These people, it is said, have failed. To avoid this failure, parents give emphasis to their children's achievement. Parents with higher levels of education, for example, usually prepare children to achieve high levels of education. Children choose careers that bring a standard of living equal to or exceeding that of their parents. Other examples are plentiful.

To achieve or accomplish, one must be able *to do* things in the form of practice, rehearse, persist, set goals, plan work, and work the plan. As a result, parents stress that their children get things done to the extent that parents consider it a symbol of children's respect for parental authority. In most homes one could regularly hear parents ask their children if they have done their work or a specific assignment. If we are required to ask our children too many times to do a task, we become frustrated because we think they are not respecting us. Some develop elaborate schemes of charts, points, stars, and rewards—all this to get children to do what we think needs to be done.

Any thoughtful person could recognize that a human being needs *to do* things and *to be* or to acquire positive personality traits. Imbalances between these may yield workers who accomplish much but have limitations to their character. People who concern themselves so much with being the right way often fail to do the necessary work and live as the hypocritical Pharisees of old who professed to be good but had few works to prove it. When we think about our ideas of success for our children, it is wise for us to direct them both *to do* the works of success and *to be* or become a person of success.

Helping Children "To Be"

There are two important reasons for us to emphasize righteous character traits as part of our parenting. Most important, of course, is the need to help children along the pathway of exaltation, which can be reached only by individuals who have developed themselves to a high level of spiritual maturity. This is referred to as perfection or completeness in our relationships with others. The second reason is less obvious. Acquiring good character traits is something every child can succeed at, because it is possible, for example, to express love or charity in many ways by everyone. All can succeed in being competent at expressing these characteristics. Parental failure to emphasize the importance of having these good traits is illustrated in the following example.

John's parents were highly educated, professional people. They had achieved awards for their scholarship, and it was understandable for them to want their children to do well and reap the same benefits. They had high expectations for all their children which were communicated through abundant praise for their successes and attention to their children's efforts. They took their children on many trips to increase their awareness of nature, people, and places. They attended school programs and participated in parent-school activities. They also communicated displeasure when a child did not perform well.

Their efforts were rewarded when their older children demonstrated achievement and followed in their parent's footsteps. John, however, was a different story than the rest. He did not show interest or ability in school work. He was very creative when it came to fixing things or making crafts in school, but he was extremely slow when it came to math, reading, and science.

One could imagine that he witnessed the praise his brothers and sisters received for their achievements. He also noticed the pleasure his parents displayed in these children. What were his feelings and thoughts when he could not succeed as they had done and knew his parents were not as happy? His suspicions about himself were probably confirmed when he was restricted to the house after failing a class. We can imagine, too, the number of times he tried to meet his parents' criteria of success and failed—so often, in fact, that by the time he was sixteen he was a confirmed failure in his own mind. He thought it, he thought his parents thought it, and they had been so busy they had done little to prevent him from thinking it so. He did not value his other areas of success, because he believed his parents did not. To survive with a little self-esteem, he rejected their values and rebelled during his teenage years. After finding the real limitations of this attempt, he improved himself, but found that his feelings of failure still nagged at him. He never seemed to realize that it was not his character that was the problem, it was the narrowness of his parents' criteria of success that created his feelings. Had he been a strong academic achiever he would have been all right. Since there was no other way to think of himself as a success, he could not and would not perhaps for the rest of his life. He committed suicide at the age of nineteen.

This true story illustrates the meaning children give to what they believe their parents consider important. Had these parents understood how to communicate their concern and their desire for their children to acquire positive character traits, their son likely would have felt differently about himself. He could have been loving, honest, and kind. They could have valued him for these and many more traits. If we want our children to be concerned about what we want them to be, we must draw their attention to the importance of positive traits, explain what they are, and teach children how to learn them.

Words which describe these traits point to less obvious human characteristics like intentions and attitudes. Since we cannot see a kind thought, for example, a different teaching technique is required than that needed to teach performance of specific tasks. Further, teaching children these traits involves numerous situations over many years, reinforced by many conversations and much parental attention.

To begin with, it is helpful to think of children's attitudes which are expressed in actions like a type of puzzle frequently seen in the *Friend* magazine. The instructions usually explain that we are to identify something like five birds, three musical instruments, an ice cream cone, and a bicycle. At the first few glances, these objects cannot be seen because they are embedded in the more obvious picture on the page. Gradually they take familiar form one by one. From this point on, our ability to spot different objects is improved because we have adjusted our visual sense and perception, plus we are encouraged by having found some of the other objects.

The inner qualities of character we want our children to have are not obvious to them, because attitudes and feelings are only indirectly observed. We infer or estimate these traits from the situation the person is in. For example, if someone helped another, we say that he or she is kind. If asked why, we could say we know this to be true because we know a kind person is helpful to others.

We must recognize that teaching our children to have these good qualities begins when they are born and takes place through our communication with them. The more we talk with and listen to them about these traits, the more accurately we will transmit an understanding of how to act to show they are learned. Of equal importance is to recognize that when we are talking to our children about their actions, they will receive, believe, and apply the positive qualities of character best when we communicate with them with warmth and consideration for them. Parents who communicate mostly in anger usually train their children to be less concerned about being "good" people. Praise, compliments, affection, and enthusiasm are necessary along with persistent attention, to ensure children receive your suggestions. There is never too much warmth and encouragement in families. Catch your children acting positively.

The first and most lasting thing we can do is develop a vocabulary of "being" words and use them in our conversation. Children learn the meanings of these words initially because of their desire to communicate with us. We can use these words when we talk about other people, when we talk about ourselves, and when we talk about our children's actions. Once we are comfortable with using the words, we can participate in a teaching program that includes informal conversations and more formal activities. A description of these can be seen in table 7.1.

Helping a Child Learn "To Do"

Some parents find it easier to require little of their children because it creates less frustration and conflict to allow them to play and do minimal work. It is also at times easier for the parents to not have to schedule, organize, and supervise their children's work. These parents often claim they get along well with their children and have a good relationship with them.

The absence of honest accomplishment in individuals' lives can be observed when these people are filled with excuses about themselves and blame others about the treatment they have received from other people. This spiritual irresponsibility is what most Latter-day Saints usually are most fearful of, and so we emphasize the importance of achievement by extolling its virtues to our children. In the New Testament, James explained that we must be doers and not hearers only (James 1:22). Mission presidents, employers, and bishops all learn to quickly identify those who will plainly and simply do the work. Such individuals have high value in the marketplace of life.

Our brains collect and sift information in order to develop our personalities and determine who and what we will be. The information collected is provided in large part by our actions, and unless we act positively we will not have enough proper information to fully form our characters as we want. The negative eternal possibilities are clear. If we fail to achieve and perform well in the effort, we also will limit the possibilities of our own growth. Therefore, the welfare of our children is enhanced when they learn to do good things and do them well.

Table 7.1
Teaching Activities for Positive Character Traits

Name of Activity	Description
1. Learn and use a "being" vocabulary.	Write a list of words which includes such descriptions as honest, loving, unselfish, warm, spiritual, considerate, caring, kind, sacrificing, willing to serve others, dependable, loyal, and trustworthy. Write an example of each and use as many as appropriate in conversation with children, pointing out examples of them in your life, their actions, or experiences of others.
2. Focus children's attention on their reasons for action.	Family life affords many opportunities to help children focus on their own attitudes and intentions. Ask, "What were you thinking before you did . . ." "How do you feel now that you have done . . ." After discussing children's motivations with them, use "being" words to describe what they *are not* (e.g., "You are not being very kind") and to describe what they *are* (e.g., "You are a very kind boy today").
3. Demonstrate living examples of the character traits.	Involve your children with you in family activities which apply knowledge of others, love for someone, and so forth. Example: (1) A Christmas project to help another family. (2) A "secret pal" program of doing nice things for each other in the family. It is children's companionship with parents that strengthens the teaching impact.
4. Dramatize positive examples of positive traits.	In family home evening, young children like to participate in dramatization of human experiences where positive traits are displayed. Follow these steps: (1) Tell the story and describe what each person did. (2) Assign parts and act it out. (3) Discuss how individuals must have felt or what they thought. Examples: The Good Samaritan, Jesus feeding the four thousand.
5. Tell personal experiences and accounts of other people's experiences.	Personal experiences and stories about other people at bedtime, mealtime, or at night with older children make lasting impressions. In chapter 3, other variations of story-telling are described.
6. Play a game called "Situations."	Describe specific situations where a child could be honest or dishonest, loving or rejecting, kind or mean, and then ask, "What is the right way to act?" A child must answer correctly before the person who is "it" counts to ten. Give bonus points if a child can explain why a certain solution would be good.

Children's abilities to organize, work, and achieve are mostly learned from the example, expectations, and encouragement of parents. This achievement motivation comes gradually in the children of involved parents. Those parents skillfully employ some specialized techniques in helping their children.

David McCleland, a Harvard University psychologist, is a pioneer in the area of achievement. In his research he found that two emotions or attitudes are involved. One is risk-taking or initiative, and the other is fear of failure. He found that children who achieved highly were able to take moderate risks and to predict successes (positive attitude) before they began. Further, if they did not succeed in their first attempt, they lowered their expectations for the next attempt until they were successful. Children who were not highly motivated to achieve predicted the possibility of failure or took unusually high risks as a face-saving ploy if they failed (which they often did). Some with fear of failure often took no risk at all (always ensuring success).

Children with fear were more tense at the start of a task, as if expecting failure. Those who expected too much and did not succeed on the first try surprisingly raised their expectations thereafter instead of making them more reasonable. Apparently, having failed the first time, they believed they should "make it up" by doing more the next time rather than adjusting their expectations. Unfortunately, this increases the likelihood of future failure.

After identifying the high- and low-achieving children, McCleland and his staff studied their parents. The results are of interest to those who want their children to feel achievement motivation and not be stopped by fears of failure (see table 7.2).

Once learned, children's achievement motivation can be channeled into several work characteristics. For example, people who learn to do tasks successfully display initiative, persist until a task is complete, organize their efforts to be most efficient, and are dependable in saying what they will do and doing what they say. There is evidence that these more specialized skills can also be taught to children (see table 7.3).

Knowing and Showing What We Want in Our Children

Many parents tell them in unmistakable ways what they want their children to accomplish in life. Others openly tell a few things

Table 7.2
Qualities of Parents of High and Low Achievers

Parents of High Achievers	Parents of Low Achievers
1. When children were young they were shown, not told how to do something.	1. Young children were more often told, not shown, what to do.
2. Parents talked about and explained the details of a task.	2. Parents often did not explain the details of a task.
3. As children grew older, parents encouraged their initiative by getting them to start tasks without parents' comments.	3. Parents either neglected their children and were uninvolved or were too involved by telling them what and how to do each task.
4. Children were asked to evaluate their own work.	4. Parents criticized their children's efforts and expressed doubt they could accomplish much of anything.
5. Parents gave children a great deal of praise and encouragement.	5. Children were praised much less often than high achievers.
6. Parents seldom criticized their children's efforts except to point out how to improve and then praised their renewed efforts.	6. Parents and children frequently argued about children's work not being done. (They inadvertently gave more attention to what they did *not* want their children to do.)

and leave the rest for the children to decide on their own. Whether we tell them or not, they will seek to understand so they can please us and because they want direction for their efforts. They learn what we want for them from what they see that pleases us, what we pay attention to in their lives, and what we teach them. Children see our actions and reactions as a natural part of family life. It is because these are often so very subtle that we need to closely examine what we communicate we want for our children. Most often they will try to be and do what they think we want.

Character traits and work habits need not be kept separate. If we leave them that way or ignore one or both, our children will not be as successful as they could be. We can integrate the two areas of success by explaining to them how doing something leads to the development of a trait. After a basketball practice, for example, one father told his sons he would rather have good boys that played basketball than good basketball players who were not good boys.

We can integrate being and doing by suggesting that a character trait is shown in what a person does. Faith, for example, is expressed

Table 7.3
Teaching Work Skills to Children

Work Skill	What Parents Can Do
Initiative	When children are young, allow exploration and movement around the house. When a child is ready, show a puzzle or game. Describe how to do it, give cues while the child does it, and praise success. Then on a new task gradually decrease your involvement but maintain praise for the child's efforts. Thereafter, reinforce what work a child does on his or her own.
Persistence and task completion	Begin a task working with the child. Then after the child is working, leave the room explaining you will return shortly to see how he or she is doing. Leaving, returning, and using unexpected rewards is the most effective way to helping children continue to work. Then focus on completion of tasks by having your children report to you when it is done; hold privileges or rewards until you and they are satisfied a task is completed.
Organization	(a) This is usually best learned as a shared activity with parents. Explain how you organize your schedule of work by "talking your thoughts." This will give your children a mental map to organize several activities. (b) Ask your children to tell you the objective of a task or the result they are trying to achieve. Discuss what your ideas are about the same idea. Being able to identify the result in advance is the most important part of organizing.
Dependability	Although this is a character trait (i.e., to be) it is closely connected to work (i.e., to do). The trait of dependability is learned through successful work being accomplished after someone has agreed to do it. Therefore, it is the consistency of follow-up and evaluations by parents after children do their work that encourages them to be dependable. If you give a task, check it over or have them mark a chart to show it is done.

by good works. We know of a doctrine after we do or live it. We must be doers, not hearers or thinkers only. It is through the results of our work (actions) that we will be known and evaluated. We can rear balanced children when we also teach them to examine their thoughts and emotions, eventually increasing self-understanding. It is true that thinking is not enough by itself without action. It is also correct that actions, even if they are correct, are not sufficient without proper intent and forethought.

In my experience one of the world's best kept secrets is that human happiness depends more on what we express and what we learn to be than on our possessions and on how we are treated by others. We can do work without learning to be righteous, but we cannot be righteous without becoming doers. Doing must therefore be the servant of being so that at the end of our lives we and our children can be like the Eternal Father of us all and live in peace and rest with Him.

8   Honesty and Identity

After Moses received the instructions from the voice in the burning bush, he was about to turn and descend the mountain when he asked the question, "When I come unto the children of Israel, and shall say unto them, The God of your fathers hath sent me unto you; and they shall say to me, What is his name? what shall I say unto them?" (Exodus 3:1-13.) The answer given to Moses was a name of the divine person who had been giving instructions to the prophets since Adam. The name seems strange to us who are used to names which tie people to nationality and to family background. The name used by Jehovah to refer to Himself described His place in the midst of all God's creations, including human beings. He said, "I Am that I Am: [tell them that] I Am hath sent me unto you" (Exodus 3:14).

These words sound peculiar to us who do not use "I Am" as a name. In our modern-day English these words simply denote being. As we think about that, however, it leads us to consider what Jehovah was communicating to us through the use of this name. I propose that He was letting us know something about a divine identity. At least He was identifying Himself as an everlasting, stable person who was, is, and will be He in whom there is good and all that is exemplary in God's order of righteousness. This is His identity. He was announcing that He had already achieved a position of completeness, a position that most of us are still striving for.

The words *I Am* acquired much greater significance to me as I interviewed a person who had done several unrighteous acts. In response to the request, "Tell me about yourself," he said without prompting: "I am *not* very religious; I am *not* as good a father as I would like to be; I am *not* able to feel comfortable around other people." As he said that he was several "I am nots," I wondered if life was different for him than for those who believed they were a collection of "am's." His life was full of fear—projects started that were not completed, unhappy experiences with others, and gaping chasms of self-doubt. He was not concerned about living a principled life that brings peace of mind. He was caught up in pettiness, suspicion, strategies and intrigues, and attempts to gain revenge. It was to me as if he were hacking away at the vines and shrubs of a jungle, wholly ignorant of an easy and beautiful path only a few feet away but obscured by self-imposed dimness of vision. He was confused about himself, and he felt inadequate.

Is the way we live influenced by what we believe to be true about ourselves? This is the great question of personal identity—one that should be of considerable interest for parents who attempt to lovingly write the law of the gospel in their children's hearts. In fact, people do live according to what they believe to be true about themselves. Beliefs formed through experience are integrated into an identity and, thereafter, our single objective is to continually reaffirm our identity by what we do. If wholesomeness and love are a part of us, we will act to make these a consistent part of life. If they are not a part of our identity but other things are, these other things will be reconfirmed by what we do. Abused children, for example, may become abusive parents because they have included in their identity the belief that this harmful treatment of children is acceptable and consequently bring this action into the next generation.

The importance of identity, what we believe about ourselves, is dramatically illustrated by some events in the Savior's life. Many of Satan's attempts to prevent the Lord from succeeding at His mission were aimed at creating doubt about His identity through the great temptations and through wicked people. Even while being crucified, Jesus was taunted, "Save thyself. *If* thou be the Son of God, come down from the cross" (Matthew 27:40; italics added). That Christ recognized that the success of His earthly life depended on our belief about His identity can be shown in the simple but marvelous question to Peter, "Whom do men say that I am?" This question is all-important to us. If Christ is who He said He is, there is an atonement for us. If we fail to believe Christ is who He said He is, we will not fully apply the Atonement and will not do all in His name. Just as it was important for Jesus to establish His identity in the minds of people who would believe, it is important for us to establish identities and help form identities in our children. Identity fuses the parts of our personality together and enables us to direct our actions toward a unified purpose. Without it, we are more aimless and confused.

The idea of identity can be understood better by thinking of a collection of puzzle pieces. We continue to think of it as a puzzle when it is in the box and while we are completing it. Once every part is in place, we no longer refer to it as a puzzle. Now that it is organized, we refer to it as a picture of something. Organization and completeness changes it. Identity is what we believe about ourselves after we understand how the parts of us fit together. We express it by thinking, "Now I am," something which suggests we have decided for ourselves and are confident our conclusion is correct. Another way of thinking about identity comes from knowing our complete range of existence from intelligence, to a spirit premortal existence, to an embodied mortal life, and finally to an exalted and glorified soul. As we gain a firm understanding of these stages we can think of our identity as eternal and express confidently, "I am a child of an eternal God."

We can gain a little more appreciation for our divine parents through our concern about identity. The human mind is a natural organizer. We do not have to consciously put things together, because our brains function to do this for us. Every experience that is ours in mortality is stored, sifted, and synthesized with the others to determine what and who we are. This is a biological inheritance given to every person. Just this alone is sufficient to lead us to think that someone with a divine purpose has prepared us beforehand to organize an identity. We can see that we and our children are prepared to experience mortal life and then have these experiences organized by our minds so that we are able to understand greater and greater spheres of true knowledge. We are of divine parentage and have been carefully prepared to grow in intelligence and wisdom, unless this is frustrated.

Why a Child's Identity Is Important

Childhood is a time of many new experiences. These may, and often do, include activities of play, of school, with friends, with family, at work, in nature, and in church. These experiences are later remembered and interpreted. Playing with friends, for example, can be interpreted as fun or unhappy. Experiences of family life can be miserable or satisfying.

As children grow older, there is a natural tendency to narrow the number of activities to a few that seem to hold the greatest promise for their future. These may be a career, a marriage, and a hobby or talent. These commitments are more long-lasting than the activities of childhood. Instead of a mere moment of activity in a child's life, we as adults invest the better part of our adult life to a few enduring patterns of behavior. We can see, then, that what we commit to as an identity will be what we usually live and participate in for the rest of our lives.

As Latter-day Saints we have some very specific ideas about what we desire in the identity of our children. These usually are formal education and acquiring knowledge in other ways, service to God and our fellowmen, and entering into an enduring love relationship with someone to create and rear a family. We believe these will endure even beyond this life. All parents want their children to have good experiences that will influence them toward these life-long objectives. Our concern is how to help them do it so their identity is formed with these experiences as the enduring parts of their lives.

At first we need to remember that children will behave throughout their lives based on what they have experienced and their interpretations of the experiences. If we wish our children to select what we believe to be eternally correct, then we must prepare them with many good experiences and help them to have a rich and positive emotional interpretation of these experiences. Two contrasting examples will illustrate.

I once had an opportunity to speak to a group of seminary teachers. As part of my presentation, I asked them to identify their five most influential experiences between the ages of twelve and nineteen. Knowing they had already chosen to be seminary teachers, one could, with a little forethought, correctly guess the kind of experiences they thought were the most important. When asked to report their selections, it was understandable that over 80 percent of the men and women reported personal experiences which had a strong emphasis in our religion and spiritual life. These experiences were then used, apparently, to enable these individuals to choose a career similar to and based on their early spiritual experiences and their interpretation of these as "most important."

The second example is about identity, but one of a less positive kind. At the time of this experience, I was a consultant to a Utah school district for the purpose of helping parents help their low-achieving children. These children were not succeeding, and most were not having pleasant experiences with school. One evening I asked this group of parents to tell of positive experiences they had had with school. No one commented. I pressed the question further and still no one spoke. I asked, "Did you not have any, or don't you remember any?" One woman said that one of her positive experiences was the warmth of the school nurse after she had fallen on the ice. We all chuckled at her story, but later a mother revealed something not at all humorous.

The children of these parents were invited to leave the room while the parents were to learn how to conduct a tutoring exercise they could use at home. As I passed the papers to them, this woman, seeing it was a spelling task, responded with disappointment, "Oh, too bad. I've never been good at spelling." The statement was spoken loud enough to be heard by several sitting near her. I encouraged her at the time, and we proceeded with the task. Later, after the children returned, the parents were asked to do the same spelling exercises with them. When this mother placed the worksheet in front of her daugher, the child looked at it, then at her mother, and said, "Oh no, I've never been good at spelling."

I could not have made up a better example of one way parents contribute to children's beliefs about themselves. These ideas believed by the mother to be true for her were clearly being transmitted to the child. If the child has both success and failure experiences with spelling, she will likely think of the failures and not the successes, because of her mother's coaching. She then will include in her identity that experience and the idea that she is "not good at spelling." The mother and the daughter are arranging for the child to have an enduring life of poor spelling. This may be the case for the child whether she is actually inadequate or not.

It is important here to reemphasize the two parts of identity formation. These are the actual experiences children have, accompanied by the interpretations of them. We parents need to be

skillful at using both. Generally it means that we do our best to pro-
vide and expose children to experiences that are consistent with what
we hope they will select as part of their identity. We all know that
learning experiences will usually lead to more religious experiences,
to future religious experiences, and so forth. The broader, the more
varied, and the richer these experiences are, the more likely they
will be used by individuals to organize an identity based on them.

The second part of identity, the interpretation children give to
the experiences, is as important as the experiences. Children have
two major sources of interpretation: our reactions to what they do,
and their reactions to what they experience. We can and should
influence both. Our positive response shown by delight in them,
continuing love, and praise are a part of what helps them interpret
themselves positively. Further, if we ask them to tell us what they
think or feel about their own experiences, it is possible to influence
their assessment if it is unduly harsh or inappropriate. Often the
more matter-of-fact we are, the more influential is our opinion. If
they seem convinced, we cannot argue and make children change
what they believe. It is valid information calmly presented by a
credible person that exerts influence. With this in mind see the
examples in table 8.1.

We can recognize that we are undergoing a process of life similar to that taken by our heavenly parents. They have an identity of
enduring qualities. When we expose our children to worthwhile
experiences and teach them a reasonable way to interpret them, the
children can then organize them into an identity of righteousness.

Honesty

It seems all right for little children to make up an exciting story
and claim it is the truth or to change the facts so they will not be
blamed for something. As they grow older, most learn a pattern of
truth or false telling, and most learn to tell the truth except for a
"white lie" or small fib now and then. These, it is reasoned, are all
right because they do not hurt anyone and sometimes one has to lie
to protect another's feelings. Whatever we believe about honesty
will usually be learned gradually until we settle on a standard that
seems to satisfy children and those around us. If we expect rigorous
honesty without demanding it, children will learn that. If we expect
lies, they will also tend to learn that.

Table 8.1
Helping Children Interpret Their Experiences

What Children Believe About Their Experiences	Suggested Parental Responses
1. A young child is afraid of something (e.g., the water, the dark, etc.).	*Respond to the feeling*—"Tell me about your feelings." Then, "Do you think being afraid is bad?" Then, "Well, some very great people have been afraid but they grew out of it. Would you like to hear about one?"
2. A young child is left out by friends.	*Sort out who is responsible*—(1) "Tell me what is happening." (2) "Why do you think this is taking place?" Help children consider what friends have done that is good and bad. Observe what the child needs to do to maintain self-respect and achieve social success.
3. A child makes a serious mistake and states that he/she is a failure.	*Gather information before arguing or disagreeing*—(1) "Well, that is interesting, I didn't know one mistake made a person a failure." (2) "Are you planning to continue being one?" (3) "I know many successes you have had, and expect you to correct this and have many more."
4. A child *fails* at school or at some task and is dejected about it.	*Recognize the failure*—After learning about the child, (1) "Yes, you have failed, and it is not a pleasant feeling." (2) "How do you think it happened?" (3) "Do you believe you can succeed if you work harder?" (4) "Do you want some help?"
5. A child quits, wants to quit, or will not start something that is hard but useful.	*Give permission to succeed*— (1) "I'm curious about why you don't want to succeed." (2) "Well, it takes hard work, so maybe that is why?" (3) "I don't want to force you, but *I think you should do it.*" (4) "Give me your reasons for not doing it even though I know you want to." (5) "What will success bring to you?"

Honesty is a character trait different from many others. It is expressed through our speech as well as our actions. When we commit acts of deception, we are expressing a lack of integrity. Honesty can be of two different types. Factual honesty is stating the facts of an incident correctly as they are remembered. Emotional honesty is expressing one's thoughts and emotions so they match the person's actions. A statement of love would be matched by actions which can be recognized as loving. Honesty is, therefore, very personal.

The importance of honesty is found in its connection with our speech. Speech is one way we present ourselves (i.e., what we really believe about ourselves) to others. Each time we talk or fail to talk we are telling something about what we think of ourselves. For example, a person engaging in stimulating, excited conversations, full of humor and enthusiasm, is telling others in an unspoken way that he or she feels happy, feels confident, and thinks the other person will like what is said. When our speech is honest, factually and emotionally, we present ourselves to others accurately and we come to trust ourselves. When we tell lies, just the opposite happens: we present ourselves dishonestly and we create mistrust for our own thoughts and feelings, even if we falsely lead others to believe what we tell them.

When we present ourselves honestly to other people and watch their response to us, their actions are more likely to be sincere. This is of great importance for our development. We can and do use other people's response or information to help us grow. For example, children will believe they are attractive and lovable only if people are attracted and loving toward them. If we present oursleves dishonestly to others, we have no right to believe their response to what we do and our development is slowed. A lying person will learn fear and mistrust of himself. He will fail in trying to achieve satisfying relationships with friends and family because the dishonesty creates suspicion about what he does or says. Honesty yields self-confidence. It is the foundation for happy marriages and successful parent-child relationships.

There is a close link between honesty and children's abilities to form an identity of positive and enduring traits. As I have stated earlier, children who learn to tell the emotional and factual truth also trust what they believe about themselves. When adolescence comes, the time for identity formation, these children will more easily organize their experiences and set their course into the future. Children who lie about the facts of some events, shift responsibility to others by blaming, and hide their feelings and attitudes in order to deceive will have greater difficulty. They will be more confused, more aimless, and less able to form close relationships with a prospective mate.

This is not what the Lord intends for His children. Nor does this diffusion lead to success here on earth. Instead, we are to prepare our children to live honestly. To speak the truth is the first requirement of a healthy and accomplished person. When this is done, children will present themselves to the world in a confident and mature way.

There are three parts to conversations that show honesty or dishonesty: (1) What children think their parents will do. (2) What children feel about themselves. (3) A description of the event or of a child's actions. It is important for parents to distinguish between the three and know how they influence children's actions. For example, children are more likely to lie if they think parents will punish severely, get extremely angry, or sharply disapprove. Since their thoughts about us influence them, we can increase their honesty potential by acting concerned and interested, but calm. Further, children will organize their statements to present a view of themselves that is positive, blameless, and whatever else they think important at the time. After listening and watching, answer the question, "How does this child think of himself or herself?" Help children find a way of telling the truth that will help them present themselves as they want to. For example, if children blame someone else for "causing" a problem, we could assume they do not want to feel small and insignificant, because they have done something wrong. We can tell them how "strong" and "important" they will be for telling the truth.

Last, the actual facts of an incident or an account of our own actions is ordinarily difficult to get exactly correct. It is the intent which is important, not the details. If we can get an accurate general understanding of some incident, it is usually enough. If we harshly judge children for missing a small fact or two, they will legitimately judge us as unfair and become more wary of us. If we see that a detail or two are deliberately left out of the description, we should try to find out why they purposely left it out. This missing information will tell us what children want and do not want to present about themselves.

Teaching Honesty

The most enduring teaching is done by example. Parents teach honesty not only by using examples and formal teaching to stress its importance but also by keeping their promises to their children and telling the truth about their own actions. When we are very honest, we can more honestly respond to the many situations children create as they grow. Some suggestions for teaching honesty are given in table 8.2.

Table 8.2
Teaching Children Honesty

Situations	What Parents Can Do
1. A child has been caught doing something wrong.	First tell the child of the importance of being honest no matter what. Then ask for his or her account of the incident. Acceptance of responsibility for his or her actions is the sign of an honest response. Separate the telling of the truth from the act itself by (a) saying the consequence will be greater if you lie, or (b) saying the consequence will be reduced if you tell the truth, or (c) rewarding telling the truth but developing a consequence for the wrong.
2. A child lies to exaggerate a personal experience.	If younger than five, ignore the dishonesty. If older, it is important to recognize the child is expressing an unfulfilled need. Do two things: (1) listen and understand what is said and how the child describes himself. That will tell you what to do to help solve the problem. (2) After saying you understand, wait a short period and ask for a retelling of the story. Rather than ridicule the changes in the child's story, ask him or her to clarify which version is correct. This clarification along with your observations is what teaches honesty.
3. A child shows strong feelings but denies them pretending nothing is happening.	Calm the child by being calm and reassuring. Ask the child to tell what he or she is feeling. You may have to ask several times and wait a while. Persist, letting the child know you know something is amiss and will not just ignore it. Listen carefully without agreeing or disagreeing and ask for the child to talk more. You may need to supply some words to help your child say what he is feeling (e.g., lonely, sad, mad, hurt, etc.).
4. A child is caught lying to avoid work or responsibility.	There are now two problems. Keep them separate: (1) the lie, (2) the need to finish the work. Explain that the lie destroys trust between you and the child and makes the child afraid. After a child is helped to admit the lie, have the child choose consequences for the lie. Then calmly insist that the child complete the work satisfactorily and afterwards help him or her to evaluate the peace that comes from honesty compared to dishonesty. Ask what will be done the next time.
5. A child is asked to tell about some incident.	Examine what a child says to ensure he or she tells about (1) their part in an incident, (2) the sequence of events (e.g., what was first, then what happened, etc.). Ask gentle, probing questions about "who did this," or "did that happen. . .?" Clearly thank children for telling the truth about what has taken place.

6. A child tells a lie to protect someone.	Congratulate the child on their willingness to be loyal, but calmly confront the child with this question: "What if you lie to me, your dad or mother, in order to protect a friend; who is the most important to you?" The objective is to teach that honoring the parental-child relationship is more important. If your relationship is not good then utilize the same approach as in situation #1 above.
7. A child is unusually silent and withdrawn.	Invite discussion by saying "I can see you are not happy; would you like to talk about something?" Examine events in the near past to see if you can identify what might have happened. Propose the event to the child to gradually get more discussion. Listen encouragingly without too much shock or anger at what you hear.
8. A child tells the truth in a situation where the temptation to lie is strong.	Reward privately by congratulations and affection. Use the example for other children to teach them the value of honesty.

Honesty Leads to a Positive Identity

The young Hebrew boy Daniel was among those of royal descent, perhaps even a prince among his people. Being without blemish, he was selected to be among those who received special education and training among the Chaldeans. He demonstrated his virtue by refusing to eat the special meat and wine provided him by the king. Apparently, he studied thoroughly, learned well, and profited from his several opportunities. At the end of his studies he was brought before the king and tested. "And in all matters of wisdom and understanding, that the king enquired of them, he found them [Daniel and his friends] ten times better than all the magicians and astrologers that were in all his realms" (Daniel 1:20).

From the richness of his experiences, Daniel formed his identity, which can be examined as an example for us to think about. We gather from his background, for instance, that he participated in many learning experiences. He learned of God and developed faith in Him. Daniel was a person of inspiration, able to understand deeply spiritual things as they were revealed to him. Daniel exhibited skill at leadership and was appointed third in the kingdom under Belshazzar and first president after Darius conquered Babylon. Even though he was conspired against, Daniel continued to pray and worship God, and as a result, demonstrated his faith while in the lion's den. Those who conspired against him did so because they could find no fault, unfaithfulness to duty, or immoral conduct. Daniel was an enduring identity to be reckoned with, for his enemies could not accomplish their purposes with him in office.

Daniel's life is impressive because the development of his faith in God, his social skill, his talents and abilities endured. They were his identity to himself and to other people. It is also clear that he had been taught to be an honest person.

If we used his life as an example of what we might do to prepare our children, we could discern several things. First, his life showed the importance of rich learning and educational experiences in which children learn academically and also through experience of what is in the world, below the world, above the world, in the past, and yet to come. Second, his life showed many experiences which involved other people. He had many opportunities to be in a variety of leadership, followership, family, and friendship situations. He was not isolated, overly aggressive, or filled with conflict. He also had been schooled in the law and teachings of God. This included praying (which he did three times daily), inspiration, a health law, and integrity. The human mind will organize identities from the activities, experiences, and knowledge of early childhood. If we wish our children to believe they are good, smart, spiritual, humorous, beautiful, hardworking, calm, kind, loving, or whatever, they must participate in receiving these early experiences and doing them. When the time comes to synthesize one's beliefs into an identity, these early experiences determine what will endure.

We must not forget, however, that it is honesty which enables the human mind to organize these various experiences into an identity which endures. If an individual has these same opportunities to learn and experience but is led into the darkness of dishonesty, then there is less assurance that the good parts of a person will last throughout life. Such individuals may live positively for a period of time, even years, but may also succumb to disintegrating experiences we think of as "mid-life" crisis or periods of lowered activity in gospel service. Latter-day Saint parents do not usually prepare children only for the events of missions or marrying in the temple. Ours is a preparation of eternal prospects. The lives of our children are made more stable and consistent when they are taught honesty and then granted the time and freedom to gain knowledge through experience. The rest is provided naturally by our intelligence.

9   Chastity, Sex, and Reproduction

It is our Heavenly Father's work and glory to prepare us for an eternal life, full and abundant. He made the concepts of life (growth and progress) and death (its opposite, physical and spiritual) recurring themes written in the scriptures. For example, we are often exhorted to choose the way of life and avoid anything death-producing. Furthermore, as we understand the concept of life we believe in successive stages of life and in preparing for the progression from one stage to another.

Our lives, a fusion of intelligence and spirit, began as an offspring of divine and exalted parents. These unembodied spirit forms combine with bodies to fulfill mortal laws and opportunities. When this form of life again changes, it is to a separation of the body from the spirit that is still learning and progressing. Finally, life in its highest form begins after resurrection.

It is clear that we are eternal beings—that in mortality our bodies are vessels of life, and that we are to learn and make choices that permit us to continue living in joy and peace. Specifically, we must learn eternal principles and apply them here.

In our premortal existence we did not have the power to act as creators of life. But having been given the right to become like our eternal parents, we have, as part of mortality, had sown within us a biological drive and a soul-felt desire to procreate. This drive and desire are inherent within the body of every mortal being, and they are divine. This means that we are to have an active role in the formation of one part of life for someone other than ourselves. Indeed, our own eternal lives may literally depend on how well we manage our power to procreate while in mortality.

Many advanced species of animal life use selection processes that in effect determine which individuals will be permitted to give life to future species members. With each season of mating, challenges and contests of strength and endurance determine the sires of the next generation. In this way the characteristics of the strong tend to be added to the species and the failings of the weak excluded.

It would not be difficult to imagine eternal, divine beings who have gone on before us and whose primary work is to procreate and foster the race of immortal beings. These eternal parents are now determined to identify those of their children who will be given the same right to create and to promote life forever and thus add to an eternal race of exalted beings. The selection process will probably not be physical, but will involve the development to perfection of the qualities the eternal parents themselves possess.

One can further reason that this process of selection for us includes how we manage the power to give life as mortal beings. Those will be chosen who keep this power within appropriate limits, using it righteously to promote the lives of others. Those who turn the power of life into selfish abuse will not be selected. It is not surprising that the greatest gift God can give is eternal procreation, the reward for the valiant, instead of wealth or power or some other blessing.

It is not difficult for one to sense that the need to protect and preserve the power to give life is one of mortality's greatest challenges. The importance of this task requires that as parents we give it our energy and emphasis in regard to our own lives and that we are responsible to prepare our children so that they may use this power and desire in a righteous manner. Our adversary wishes to prevent us from succeeding and encourages the improper use of this power so that the precious work of our eternal parents will be frustrated. For it is true that every abuse of the power to give life leads in the direction of death, the inability to procreate. Promiscuous sexual behavior often results in disease that can permanently destroy procreation. Other sensual pleasures such as drug abuse can destroy and alter the genetic composition of offspring, making the continuation of life more difficult.

Responsible Latter-day Saint parents who wish to be righteous must teach children how to properly manage this life-giving power. This must be done to ensure the preservation of our eternal families.

Unfortunately, we too often neglect this. I have informally asked some of my students at BYU how many had parents who contributed to at least 50 percent of their knowledge about sex and reproduction. In the years I have taught, never more than 20 percent of the students have indicated they learned more from their parents than from someone else. In 1985, I asked a class of 247 students this question. By actual hand count, 23 students indicated they had learned more than 50 percent from their own parents. If we are not doing the teaching, then who is doing it? If we are not teaching what we want our children to know, what are they learning? I, for one, do not like to contemplate the many negative possibilities of some television programs, misinformed friends, or pornographic literature.

Chastity

Latter-day Saints believe in being chaste. We want our children to be chaste and to avoid the misfortune that results from immoral sexual behavior. Many of us also know that the most effective way for children to learn chastity is through the teachings of involved parents. Yet, as I have suggested, a majority of parents teach neither about chastity nor about sex and reproduction. The reasons we do not are probably threefold. First, it can be a sensitive subject that is uncomfortable for us to talk about. Second, at the times we are faced with needing to say something, we do not know for certain if it is best to give children sexual information and risk their experimentation or keep them naive and risk their exploitation by some predatory person. Third, we often do not have a clear idea about what chastity means and how children should develop it. We often believe it is merely the absence of sexual activity. So if our children are not actively engaged it is easy to assume that they are chaste and that nothing more is required of us.

In this day, however, we are faced with rearing children amid a great deal of generally available, explicit sexual information. We need to develop a method of teaching that works and is appropriate for these times. This will allow us to be the primary teachers of our children without risking their improper experimentation.

I believe the development of a teaching plan requires a set of operating principles that we can use with our children. The first principle, I believe, is that chastity is primarily a spiritual and mental condition, and its application is sexual. Most of true chastity is the attitude of reverence for life, respect and care for self and others, and a virtuous love. Chastity is learned. Since it is an attitude as much as it is sexual actions, it is violated at the mere thought of exploiting another for selfish reasons. One does not have to participate in sexual relations to become unchaste. This idea is not commonly believed or taught. Most young people, for example, think that chastity is simply avoiding sexual intercourse. Other forms of sexual behavior are all right, according to this belief, as long as intercourse is avoided. I believe it is better to understand that being chaste is maintaining an attitude of respect, modesty, and care for the welfare of another person.

Growing out of this attitude is the recognition that chastity is positive and rewarding. We often say to children that they should not think certain thoughts, not touch parts of their own bodies except under appropriate conditions, not speak certain words, not let others touch them in restricted places, and not touch others in these same places. Quite often in our attempts to teach them what not to do, children learn their very thoughts and desires are as bad as improper sexual conduct. Many reared in this atmosphere learn guilt and inhibition and take them into marriage because they have the notion that any sexual impulse is wrong.

Instead, chastity is simply the best way to prepare for an exciting, warm, and passionate marriage relationship. The feelings and thoughts of sexual desire are a wonderful part of life, divinely placed within each worthy person. They are to be regulated before marriage in order for people to prepare for the best sexual experience after marriage and to develop the ability to make lasting emotional commitments. There is mounting evidence that those who participate in premarital sexual activity are more likely to be insecure about love and commitment, resulting in a reduced ability to establish an enduring relationship with another person.

It is also important to understand that the more completely we can express ourselves the happier we will be. Restriction or inhibition constricts the soul and limits our sensation of peace and contentment. Of course, restriction and inhibition should not be confused with self-denial. Self-denial is control of impulses at inappropriate times in order to more fully express them at another time. To achieve this, certain conditions must be created to allow this full expression. For example, premarital sexual conduct is not bad only because we are giving or expressing too much at an inappropriate time but also because it prevents us from being able to give all that we wish to give. We cannot, with premarital sex, give the promise of lasting love shown by a marriage covenant. We cannot give the security of fidelity in the future if we live separately except for sexual union. We cannot share the full joys of parenthood together, should that result, if we are not joined in a lasting lawful relationship.

These points of thought were dramatically illustrated during an interview I had with a young couple. "She's pregnant," he said as we entered the room. "We want to know what we should do." There was no need to examine how, when, or why it happened, so we talked about the alternatives for their future. He had been preparing for a mission and still wanted to go. She had just graduated from high school and wanted to go to college.

"Have you been thinking about an abortion?" I asked in order to build a case against that soul-darkening practice all too common in our day. "No," they both replied. "I'm glad," I told them. "Your problems would be made far worse if you did that." We talked more about why abortions are harmful, and then we considered what else might be available to them. It is easy to see how their situation prevented the full expressions of feeling and responsibility.

We talked of telling their parents and proposing they get married. To this idea he stated that would eliminate his mission plans. He would have to work full-time to support a wife and child, and she likely would have to work both before and after the child's birth in order to meet living expenses. Her college education would be forfeited unless their parents would help them financially. His parents couldn't, I was told, and hers wouldn't because they did not like him very much and would not like him at all if they found out about their situation. "Besides," she said, "I don't know if I love him enough to get married. How do you know?" she asked rhetorically.

I suggested then that they break up so that she could have the baby with her parents' support, care for it by herself until he finished his mission, and then perhaps they could get together when both were older and more ready. She responded that this idea seemed unfair because she would have to have and raise the baby alone without any support or help from him. "Besides," he said, "it is my baby, too, and I would want to be its father."

I could see that the full impact of their situation was being felt, and I dreaded bringing up the next possibility. But I have learned it is best for people in this situation to get a clear understanding of reality. "You could," I began, "separate because you are not ready or able to marry, have the baby, and place it for adoption." This possibility is one often taken, but it hurts. He began to weep. "That would mean I'd never know my child," he said. She sat, head down and slumped, not able to put her thoughts into words. Finally, after a prolonged silence, he asked, "What would you advise?" I told them the best of these alternatives was to consider marriage and try to find parental help. They could have their child and, with help, obtain an education. They left my office undecided but with a promise to tell their parents as soon as possible. Later, I learned they had separated.

It is chastity that allows us full expression of all that is deep and profound within us regarding children. It is unchaste sexual activity that prevents and inhibits our abilities. Premarital sexual activity prevents those involved from giving all within them to their committed partner.

Lastly, we need to understand that chastity, if lost, can completely be regained again. Some mistakenly think that if they make a mistake once they are permanently sullied and it does not matter what they do after that. They also believe they will never be free from the guilt and shame. Both ideas are wrong. One mistake does not reduce chastity as much as two or more. Further, through the Lord's atonement and at considerable cost in repentance, chastity can be fully regained. Men and women all should, in my opinion, be taught this at the same time that they learn of the great pain and great effort required to regain chastity.

The Teaching Plan

I found that when my children grew older and more inquisitive, I had difficulty answering their questions. I had considered reproduction as sexual only and I had learned to associate talking about sex as an immodest or undesirable activity. For this reason I did not talk very freely about it, nor did I spend much time reading about how to present this information to children. I was embarrassed and hesitant when times came to answer specific questions. I found myself doing what many parents do, which consisted of avoiding it as much as I could. But my attitude changed when I began to think of teaching my children about the gifts and powers of creating life in its eternal perspective. This was in contrast to thinking of it only in mechanical sexual terms. Further, I realized that to neglect teaching my children was to risk turning their education about this important matter over to other influences that may not be depended upon to do it as my wife and I wanted. This possibility was reinforced when our two oldest children had negative experiences because of some pornographic pictures shown to them by friends. It became clear that as parents we were in a contest with other forces for the education and attitudes of our children. External influences could not be successfully eliminated, so the right course seemed to require that we learn how to teach about life and reproduction, do it regularly, and do it before ideas from undesirable sources reached our children.

Attitudes and values about something are most often learned by how we choose to teach more than what is taught. For example, if a parent teaches sexual information in an embarrassed or nervous way, there is a good chance children will assimilate these same feelings about sex. Or, if parents believe sex is evil and view it as base and animalistic, these attitudes may also be communicated. This implies that the first step in teaching children needs to be a preparation of ourselves. This preparation can begin with an evaluation of how successfully our children learn or will learn the attitudes of chastity. These usually are learned gradually and will take as long as our children are with us. Also we can learn to say the names of the parts of the male and female anatomy and can practice until we feel comfortable doing so with our children. Someone suggested to me that I turn on the shower and say these words out loud until I felt no embarrassment. I laughed when I heard this, but it turned out to be a fairly good suggestion.

It is important to identify the objectives of our teaching plans. I believe that one objective should be to form a relationship with our children in which both parents and children freely talk whenever either wishes to do so. The discussion of sex and reproduction can be used to improve a relationship. Being able to freely talk is a prerequisite to teaching values. Subsequently, whenever our children ask questions, we can first praise them for coming to us and then try to tell them what they want to know.

In addition to wanting them to have an accurate factual knowledge about sex, another objective is to have our children learn from both parents if both are available. There is much sons *and* daughters can and should learn from both parents. A third goal is to teach some things at different times depending on a child's readiness to learn. Lastly, in addition to believing that sex is a source of joy in this life, I believe we want our children to have a deep understanding that the power of their bodies to create mortal life is a sacred trust, and that expressing sexual love regularly and properly is necessary to form an eternal bond between husband and wife. To understand this they must avoid seeing sexual impulses as something to only be repressed. They must learn that they need to control themselves as a means of preparing to make a relationship with a marriage partner the best it can possibly be.

One cannot have the fullest sexual experience when appropriate if there are not times when sexual desire is constrained. Not having something pleasurable at one time increases the intensity when experienced at another time. There is evidence that the best sexual relationships in marriage are those in which people live standards of sexual behavior consistent with our values as Latter-day Saints. That is, sexual behavior with someone only occurs in a context of deep emotional commitment for the purpose of procreation or of bonding two people together. Suggestions for what to teach and methods for teaching it can be seen in table 9.1.

A Lifetime of Teaching

There are some moments when we clearly see and feel that our family is eternal. During these times it is as if the obstacles to our understanding are removed, the veil thinned, and a glimpse offered into other worlds. Sometimes, however, we are so involved with other things that we misplace our attentions and fail to understand that we can have a parental relationship with our children forever. It is during these times that we miss the teaching moments and fail to see future consequences for what we do or don't do. For example, successful management of sexual desires during adulthood requires that we learn control of emotional impulses while still young. Many of us will mistakenly allow our young children to have tantrums, to

Table 9.1
Suggested Teaching Program

First Concepts in Childhood (Ages 0-7)

Developmental Stages of Children's Understanding	Concepts That Parents Can Teach	Suggested Ways to Teach
Young children are curious and think about objects and their physical properties such as shape, texture, size, and color. Children also organize ideas into concepts (e.g., what parts does a boy or a girl have). They want to know about sensations and their feelings.	1. Teach about body parts (using correct terms) and about differences between males and females. 2. Teach when to talk about parts of the body and when not to. 3. Teach concepts of modesty and how wonderfully our bodies are made. 4. Begin principles of conception, pregnancy, and child prenatal growth. 5. Teach about life, its beauty, and how helpfulness towards others makes life better.	1. Use baths or showers and children's questions as times to teach about the body. 2. Verbally explain when it is best to talk. 3. Use examples and positive comments about your own body and the child's body to teach modesty and self-respect. 4. Use reading materials about prenatal growth and childbirth. Use own pregnancy if appropriate. 5. Be loving, touch, and give affection.

Emotional Control and Prepuberty
Physical Development (ages 7-11)

Developmental Stages of Children's Understanding	Concepts That Parents Can Teach	Suggested Ways to Teach
From ages 7 to 11 children learn the sense of relationships to other people and learn to control emotions associated with personal life and social contacts. They are interested in understanding reasons why things take place. They are interested in social friendship skills. Children often experiment out of curiosity. This may include kissing, showing genitals, or infatuation.	1. Teach about conception (sperm and egg unite) and reproduction. 2. Reinforce the need for children to talk openly with parents about questions. 3. Use social events to teach modesty and appropriate conversation. 4. Help children learn to regulate their emotional impulses, to avoid extreme or uncontrolled displays, and to be loving, touch, and give affection. 5. Teach the concept of self-respect and respect for others. 6. Be explicit about what touching and affection is proper. 7. Teach how people can hurt one another through selfishness.	1. Initiate conversation to learn about what a child knows. Reinforce your need to have the child talk to you. 2. Respond to questions as asked. 3. When a child exhibits extreme emotions, focus on the need to manage his feelings. Emphasize that each child is responsible to control the expression of his emotions. 4. If children ask about their conception, tell about it forthrightly as a loving union between a father and mother.

Puberty and Early Adolescence
(Ages 11-15)

Developmental Stages of Children's Understanding	Concepts That Parents Can Teach	Suggested Ways to Teach
1. Increased interest in the body and in relating a person's body to such things as popularity, athletic skill, and attraction to opposite sex. Increased awareness of physical changes and comparing themselves to others. They notice voice change, breast development, height, and hair on the body. 2. Increased self-consciousness about looks and ability to relate how they look to other things such as others' respect and social values. 3. More importance is given to opinions of peers. 4. Children experience strong sexual desire for the first time. 5. Children can mentally see the logic behind reasons; they perceive cause and effect relationships.	1. Teach about the changes that occur in puberty (i.e, menstruation, rapid growth that can be related to poor coordination, a widening of shoulders and narrowing of hips for boys, widening of hips for girls, enlargement of breasts for both boys and girls, development of body hair under arms, in pubic area, and on boys' faces and arms.) 2. Teach that good looks do not make a good person and that one must develop good values, standards of personal conduct, and modesty. 3. Teach social skills (how to make friends, talk with others, and achieve success) so that popularity can be achieved on some basis other than physical attraction. 4. Teach that individuals go through puberty at different ages and rates—some early, some late, some rapidly, some slowly. Teach that our bodies and spirits are God's greatest earthly creations, and to respect ourselves is to respect Him. Teach how hormones change in the menstrual cycle, and increase and decrease sexual desire. Teach that self-abuse through masturbation will result in loss of self-esteem and feelings of self-doubt. 5. Ask them how they will demonstrate concern for others, service to others, and love for others.	1. Reinforce changes in children as positive by attention to their growth ("You sure have broad shoulders"). Create teaching times in which children are told what to expect for boys and girls during puberty. 2. Initiate numerous conversations to ensure development of positive attitudes about a child's body, social success, and personal standards. 3. Share some of your own experiences with puberty and its changes. 4. Teach ways to manage sexual desire (e.g., avoid pornography, become involved in physical work, conversation about feelings, and thought control). 5. Frequently ask what ideas your children have about themselves. Obtain good reading and other information to use with your family.

Late Adolescence
Ages 15-18

Developmental Stages of Children's Understanding	Concepts That Parents Can Teach	Suggested Ways to Teach
1. Children can observe how they relate to others.	1. Teach relationship of sex as a commitment to another person in marriage.	1. Share personal experiences showing correct choices.
2. Reasons and ideas must appear logical to be accepted.	2. Too much sexual involvement too early cheapens and can ruin the companionship.	2. Ask children to tell you their decisions about chastity. Ask, "What have you decided to do?"
3. Perceived ability to make their choices is necessary for development of personal values. Attempts to force ideas will evoke resistance.	3. Physical attractiveness used to increase popularity will achieve temporary results. Personality and skills will result in more permanent success.	3. Emphasize positive examples of young people marrying properly.
4. Social success increases in importance, especially attention from the opposite sex. Personal esteem is closely tied to feelings of being socially successful.	4. How to hold expressions of intimacy within appropriate limits according to the state of responsible and legal commitment.	4. Initiate long talks about affection, sex, and relationships with others.
5. Children require abundant positive emotional support from parents.	5. Sexual desire well managed is a major part of preparing for success in marriage.	5. Express confidence, support, and love.
6. Although children can understand correct principles, most have difficulty acting according to what they believe.	6. Techniques for avoiding compromising situations. This can be done for both males and females.	6. Tell children clearly what you want for them and why without demanding or threatening.
	7. Teach the consequences of inappropriate sexual behavior.	7. Avoid critical comments about their looks, choices, or actions. Instead focus on desirable things you want them to do.
	8. Teach the characteristics of chastity and ask them to evaluate themselves.	

believe they can get whatever they want, or to be undisciplined in work and achievement. When the time comes for them to restrain themselves from inappropriate behavior, these children do not have internal controls and are more susceptible to temptation. Furthermore, when a child does not have internal controls, he or she uses the influence of others to determine the choices that he or she makes. These reasons sound like "everyone else is doing it," "I will lose him if I don't," or "we were carried away."

All of these reasons suggest that personal choices are not as strong as external influences. The children who abuse their sexual desires often feel this is the case. Every child needs to know regularly from early on that he is responsible to decide for himself and will face the consequences of what he chooses. There is no such thing as seduction of one person by another. There is only a failure to decide for oneself or a willingness to participate shown in small relinquishings of standards over a period of time. In either case, each person is responsible to choose, to act, and to realize the results. In my opinion, helping children learn this one idea ought to be a major focus of every parent for as long as parents and children associate.

When we more fully realize that life is forever and our children will always be significant to us, we can see our roles changing but never becoming unimportant. Children deserve to see parents live exemplifying principles of modesty, continence, and fidelity. They also deserve to learn more from their parents than from anyone else. Moreover, to succeed they must see the joy that living these principles brings in contrast to the dullness of life resulting from inappropriately using the power to create. Parenthood is truly a lifetime of teaching.

10   The Family Practice

Scripture contains accounts of individuals coming into mortal life with a special purpose attached to their time here. One such person was Joseph Smith, who was sent here to be the great prophet of the final gospel dispensation. Another was the prophet Jeremiah, who was sanctified and ordained a prophet before he was formed in the womb. Our first father, Adam, as Michael the angel of God, participated in the creation of the world and in preparation for his role as the earthly father of all mankind. In fact, we are told in the Book of Mormon (Alma 13) that many faithful men were called and ordained before this life to bear the priesthood of God on earth in order to teach God's commandments to the children of men.

This idea of foreordination is well known to Latter-day Saints. The best example, of course, is the Savior, whom we know in his roles as the firstborn Son of God, as Jehovah of the Old Testament, and as Jesus the Christ, the Messiah, awaited since the beginning of time. Jesus Christ, Adam, Jeremiah, and Joseph Smith were all priesthood holders blessed or foreordained with special missions to be carried out at the time of their mortal lives.

Each of us may be sure that our premortal conditions, experiences, and choices influence the opportunities we have in mortality. On this earth such opportunities can be revealed to us personally or expressed or emphasized in special priesthood blessings, especially in the patriarchal blessing sought by worthy members of the Church.

It is clear that correctly predicting what a person will be like and what he will do is possible if the person chooses to honor the laws upon which the experiences and blessings are predicated. As

believing parents we can apply this principle in seeking to understand how the tendencies our children exhibit will be expressed in
their future lives. More important, we may be (and I believe we are)
in a position to increase the likelihood that our children will succeed at some things important to us. Most of us want to know how
to exert influence in a way that results in children choosing to do
and to be those things we value highest. The most difficult part of
being a parent is deciding what will help accomplish this and what
will not. This task is complicated because what seems to work with
one child does not always work with another.

We often approach this task by first evaluating what our parents did and determining whether we can use those things. If we do
not like the way our parents were, we promise ourselves never to
do to our children what our parents did to us. Often, however, we
find we do exactly what our parents did, or else just the opposite,
which also yields failure. To some degree, every generation of parents is unique, but we are like our parents in many ways, too, for
they are our primary example.

Good decisions about what to do to promote children's success
are based on good information. Knowing what our parents did or
did not do can be useful. More useful, however, is understanding
how a family exerts influence on children and the relationship between
children in a family and children as they move into our society.

In a conversation after church one day, a man raised an interesting question. "If," the question began, "an infant is not capable of
understanding a father's blessing, what good does it do to give those
blessings at such a young age?" My friend's answer was of great
interest to me because it illustrated the role families generally have
in the lives of children. "I have often thought," he said, "that the
blessing was for the people in the circle. They are usually close relatives, perhaps home teachers, and priesthood leaders. In other words,
they, along with female relatives in the audience, are the primary
caretakers of the child." He continued by saying that the blessing is
given to the infant, but those giving it will see that it is realized. I am
not sure if this answer is wholly correct, but I thought his idea was
interesting. The caretakers do help make blessings come true for
children, or they help prevent these blessings from being realized.

The Family Environment

There are, as we all know, many types of families. There are as many different kinds as there are varieties of ways for parents to supply leadership. In all families, however, learning takes place; and family life, good or bad, is the primary source of what children think, feel, and do. More than friends or school or church or any other social group, families shape children's lives. Knowing the way families exert this influence will help us organize our own families to encourage children to become what we would like them to become.

Understanding how children are influenced is fairly easy if we begin by accepting a few ideas about family life. First, a family is a group in which children learn a "range of tolerance" for their behavior. If children's actions are acceptable to parents (or older children), children will feel confident to continue their actions. If their actions are not acceptable, they will find it necessary to change what they are doing. If the range of tolerance is broad, parental discipline will be more flexible than it will be if the range is very narrow.

Second, relationships among family members usually involve feelings which are more intense than those felt anywhere else. Spoken words and patterns of actions are more primary (that is, children are affected earlier and more profoundly) than in other relationships. Children learn to survive in the world of people with emotions by their experience in the family.

Third, families develop a style of communicating complete with ways of speaking, showing signs, and interpreting symbols that will determine how children learn to process information. Some families share a great deal of information; others confer only at certain times about certain topics; still others share very little information at all. The amount of information a family uses has a great effect on what children become. Families who share very small amounts of information, for example, usually have children who are more fearful of social activities and less productive in school and at work. Parents in these families usually resort to an autocratic form of discipline. Some families share moderate numbers of ideas, usually those that support parental values. Parents are more likely to employ a democratic form of leadership in this situation, and the children are more goal-oriented, have higher levels of achievement, and are more confident socially.

Fourth, once family relationships are formed, no one is free to be indifferent to what happens. The family rules, the relationships, and the communication style become a universe of understanding that includes all who are members of the family. Our thoughts about ourselves, the way we present ourselves to other people, our values, and our beliefs about the world are shaped by this little universe. This takes place in many ways, in many situations, usually over the long period of the vulnerable years of early childhood. This makes families the root of our personal life.

When infants enter families they are usually intelligent and attentive. They are capable of imitating facial expressions, recognizing familiar voices, and using all their senses to learn. Their caretakers play with them, touch them, and talk to them. Even though an infant does not respond at the level of maturity of the stimulation it receives, it immediately begins to learn about human relationships. It begins to become what it will be.

What follows is a complex set of situations in which the children learn in order to maintain contact with their parents. They learn physical skills, to talk, to imitate, and to adapt to what they believe will win positive parental contact for them. Many parents are familiar with a four-year-old asking what seems an endless number of "why?" questions. We tend to think this indicates children's curiosity. But if we realize what these questions accomplish for children, it is clear that this is a way for children to keep their parents involved with them. Involvement with adult caretakers is so important to children that often they will adapt their personalities in order to perpetuate it. A child with a controlling parent may learn to be dependent. Another, with parents who are critical and disapproving, may become fearful and indecisive. Happily, of course, children may also become loving in order to participate with loving parents. There are many other such examples.

While these relationship adaptations are taking place, children gradually increase their time and participation in activities outside the home. This means that what is learned at home will be tested and applied with other people. The way children believe about themselves and other family members forms a mental map they use to chart their course in life. Children meet successes when their family experience has prepared them well, or they meet failure if they find that what was learned at home was not useful. Some children find that family and society reflect the same values which makes the transition from home to the adult world relatively easy. Some dismiss the outer world and retain family values. Others find external social experiences better and reject the family. Still others will have conflict between the two and have trouble for a period of time trying to decide which they will follow.

The Family Learning Environment

Children's increasing participation in external social activities can give us two important opportunities if we are alert to them. The first is an understanding of what our children might do in the future. The second and more important one is the privilege to exert influence and guidance based on our relationship with each child.

To explain further I offer the following example. A ten-year-old girl at school was observed to spend 80 percent of her time with adults and 20 percent of her time with children her own age. Her parents felt this to be inappropriate and asked the school counselor to help. The counselor helped the girl make a commitment to spend 80 percent of her time with friends and 20 percent of her time with adults. Then he invited her into his office one hour each week and asked her to talk about playing with her friends. He praised her as she talked, and soon she talked of nothing but her activities with friends.

The problem in the situation is easily seen. Though the girl spent more time talking about her friends, the actual percent of the time she played with her friends did not change. In fact, while she was talking about playing with her friends, she was in the presence of an adult. Like many parents, the adults in this example were doing exactly what would ensure the child to fail. All the while, the little girl thought herself to be more successful in meeting the demands of these adults, she was perpetuating the pattern they considered inappropriate.

This leads us to two principles of organization that influence how our children will perform elsewhere.

1. We must first learn what our children need to be able to do or how they need to act in a situation in order to be a success. (Note: if children fail to succeed in a situation outside the family they will have less desire to continue in it.)

2. The learning environment of the family must match what we
   want to happen, or it must require behavior similar to that
   needed for children to succeed in a setting outside the home.

We can now see how these two principles are applied. We can
consider the relationship between our families and church activities,
for example. Fortunately, there are a variety of ways to be successful
as a Latter-day Saint. Successful involvement in church activities,
however, requires that we know how to do some fairly specific
things. One is to give talks. Another is to read adequately in private
and public. Another is to pray vocally before a group. Still another is
to adjust from leader to follower and back again if required. In addition, we are more successful if we know scriptural stories and basic
points of doctrine or belief. We might also include "teaching" as
something that every successful Latter-day Saint does. These and
other acts like them can be part of what we hope our children will
learn. Knowing these, having them in our minds, satisfies the first
principle of the learning environment.

These more social aspects of our religion (as contrasted to the
private spiritual aspects) are important because feeling comfortable
with them enables us to more fully participate in our religion. Confidence in these skills as part of religious practice helps children feel
accepted and wanted. It is not surprising, then, that young people
who cannot read well or who have difficulty with public speaking
or are shy about participation in a class may avoid situations where
these are required, and therefore would tend to be less active in
church.

If we think of our family as the environment for learning those
skills, we can develop family activities that will teach children to
perform the actions that lead to success at church by matching what
we do in our family to what children must do elsewhere. This is the
second principle of the family learning environment. Suppose parents organized their family home evening to have their children take
turns conducting, teaching a lesson, displaying talents, giving talks,
or leading games. These would be family activities that match the
actions required for success in church.

My family has followed this type of plan. Over the years we
have helped our children develop several skills, including giving

extemporaneous talks, leading the singing, and conducting a meeting. I saw the tremendous impact of the family learning environment when one of my sons forgot that he was scheduled as a youth speaker in sacrament meeting. He remembered on the way to church. In our family talent nights the children were taught to speak without notes and to follow a general outline: (1) tell the audience what you are going to talk about, (2) give some reasons why it is important to them, (3) tell an illustrative story, (4) explain how the audience can use the idea, and (5) close the talk.

Remembering, this son said, "Dad, tell me a story, quick!" I could not think of one right away, and the more excited he became the less I was able to concentrate. As we arrived at the chapel I remembered a story about my grandfather who had an answer to a prayer when in great need. As Grandfather was walking toward his home after praying in solitude, a man came toward him and said, "Young man, what do you need?" This man, a bishop, had been sitting in a meeting and said that he felt inspired to go to my grandfather who was walking down the street and help him.

After I told this story to my son, we hurriedly went into church. He walked to the stand, and I sat with the rest of my family. When it was time for him to speak, he followed the outline he knew well and gave an excellent talk, without notes, about being sensitive to the Spirit of the Lord. He suggested to the audience that they could be as sensitive as was the bishop in the story. What made this experience an example of the family's learning environment happened after the meeting. People gathered around this boy and praised his efforts (some his preparation), which made him feel successful and accomplished. They could not know that the immediate preparation for this talk took about three minutes. Of course, the actual preparation had taken place over the years during "talent night" in our home. Watching the praise my son received after his talk at church, I had no fears about his future activity; he would return where he was liked and appreciated.

It will be obvious that this idea applies equally well to our efforts to help children succeed in school, at parties, during meals with others, in conversations, and during dating and courtship. All we must do is find what actions lead to success in a setting and then practice them naturally in our families. Children need not know they are being prepared. Parents may find it necessary, as I have done, to go and observe or to go and ask someone in order to find out what works successfully in each situation children will encounter.

The actions that lead to success in many common settings are well known. As a reminder, we can consider the results of research as shown in table 10.1. We can add to children's success by organizing activities or otherwise involving them in the practice of these actions.

The second guideline for the family learning environment suggests that our family life include opportunities for children to practice in the family the actions that match the actions of success. There are many creative ways for parents to involve children. It is part of what makes parenting fun.

Table 10.1
What Leads to Success

The Setting	Successful Actions
1. School	(1) Keeping eye to eye contact with the teacher. (2) Asking questions, getting answers. (3) Completing tasks. (4) Thinking of ways to organize work. (5) Hearing and following three directions in sequence. (6) Showing recognition of learning. (7) Showing attentiveness.
2. Social Relationships	(1) Giving compliments. (2) Sharing toys, food, expense for activities. (3) Cooperating while performing work. (4) Balancing talking with listening. (5) Developing well a talent that can be expressed in public. (6) Expressing warmth and care to others through concerned statements, modest touch of hands and arms, and affection. (7) Voicing opinions about what one thinks and believes. (8) Developing the ability to say a gracious "no." (9) Avoiding gossip.
3. Work	(1) Being punctual. (2) Doing extra than required without being asked. (3) Talking and listening actively and other conversation skills. (4) Making decisions effectively. (5) Organizing or setting priorities in work. (6) Setting goals.

Family Conversations

It has been asserted that we think with the words we know, or the ideas that the words represent. The more words we know, the richer are our ideas. This powerful idea, if even partly correct, tells of another way families influence what children eventually become. We will see that families influence what children think and then do by the way the family members communicate with one another. For example, one woman I know said that she was never satisfied by anything she did. There always seemed to be an inner voice saying that she could do more or do something better. "Whose voice is it?" I asked. After answering, "Mine," and then thinking about it, she said, "No, I never realized it before, but it is my mother's voice—always critical, never praising."

Our family conversations, the words we say and the actions we show while we talk, play a major role in determining the quality of a family's time together and also in forming a way of thinking which children carry into their lives after leaving home. It is well known, for example, that hearing swearing at home can lead to swearing elsewhere, or that the size of a parent's vocabulary and ease of speaking are often reflected in the way children later express themselves.

But there are some things about the way we converse with each other that are more subtle than these examples yet still have a powerful effect on how children come to think and act. If we know about and use these devices correctly, we can better lead our children to think, decide, and live according to what we value most.

Our values are displayed in the amount of influence we share about them. I remember well the beginning of my awareness of an important value my mother had that had a great impact on my life. I used to come in late from the fields of my father's farms after the evening meal had been long since cleared away. This particular evening I came in about ten o'clock, and as was my mother's custom, food had been warming. After she set the meal for me to eat, she began to tell me of a book she was currently reading. It was *Plutarch's Lives*, a book about the lives of ancient statesmen—philosophers like Cicero and Solon. In the small kitchen of a remote farm house, this mother was telling me, her son, about the ideas of these people. I listened with interest, as I usually did when my mother

talked. Mother had a great way of telling things, transporting a lis-
tener as if to the very spot of a historical event, movie episode, or
romantic intrigue. I have reflected on that night and the many others like it and wondered what motivated my mother.

As I grew older I put together several bits and pieces of information. One was that Mother had quit school after the seventh
grade. Her father had gone blind and, as an older child, Mother had
to work to help support her family. She and Dad, who was only
able to finish the eighth grade, loved books. They read often and
talked about what they read. All of their children have graduated
from college, and three of the six have advanced degrees. For all of
us, going to college seemed as inevitable as breathing. It was simply
what the children in this family did. There was no pressure to go.
Mother and Dad gave no persuasive lectures that I can remember.
We all seemed naturally to prepare for it with the same enthusiasm
Mother showed for knowledge and learning.

What we value highest takes form in our family goals or projects.
We try to bring information into the family that supports our values
and screen out what does not. Some parents do not allow much
information into the family, and their children develop a narrow
and prejudiced view of people and institutions. Other families screen
nothing out and find their children experimenting with the sensa-
tional. Parents can assess what they consider important and how
well they suppport it by considering what magazines and newspa-
pers they subscribe to and read, what kinds of television programs
or movies they watch, what kinds of activities they encourage their
children to participate in. What children enjoy with their parents
will become prominent aspects of their decisions and interests later
on.

Besides the amount and kind of information families use in
their communication, another aspect of family conversations that
exerts influence on children's future is the use or function of the
language itself. Seven different functions of language have been identified. It is possible to recognize situations outside the family which
require use of each of these language functions. These situations,
along with a description of the seven language uses, may be seen in
table 10.2.

Table 10.2
Seven Language Functions and Situations for Their Use

Language Function	Description	Situations When Language Function Is Required
1. Regulating	Telling others what to to do, organizing, and controlling. Example: "Stop that." "Get going."	Leadership positions, parenthood.
2. Instrumental	Organizing, planning, and achieving. Example: "We need a pencil in order to write a paper."	Any situation that requires work–school, household chores, or career achievement.
3. Discovery	Gathering information, finding out why things happen, expressing curiosity. Example: "Why?" "How come?"	Science or any attempt to learn about people or things.
4. Personal	Disclosing information about oneself. Example: "I am happy." "I am going to be a fireman."	Any experience one participates in that calls for telling one's thoughts and feelings. Some examples are religion, intimate relationships (like marriage), friendships, etc.
5. Interpersonal	Discussing one's relationship with another. Example: "I love you." "We are good friends, aren't we?"	Any social situation whether with a group of people or one individual. These statements show the speaker understands what goes on between himself and another or others.
6. Information	Giving factual information. Example: "The wind blew the tree over."	Virtually any conversational situation which calls for discussion of past, present, or future.
7. Imaginative	Fantasy, fiction, dreams, and hopes. Example: "Once upon a time there was a princess . . . "	Storytelling, creative experiences like music or art, acting or writing.

All seven types of statements are usually used in family conversations. Some language functions, however, become more prominent than others in a particular family. This will influence children in their relationships with people from other families. We might find, for example, that a girl who has grown up accustomed to using personal and interpersonal language may yearn for companionship and intimate conversation with a husband whose family emphasized information and instrumental parts of language. Consequently, he may seem to lack an ability to talk about personal thoughts and feelings, or even an awareness of her feelings and desires. Other examples of this phenomenon include people who dream and hope but fail to actually achieve; they may come from families where instrumental language was seldom employed in conversations. On the other hand, children from creative families, who learned creative language, may continue to show this ability as part of their careers.

The point of all this is to assert that parents can, with some planning, influence what children might eventually do. There is no absolute guarantee that our language style strictly determines children's later choices; it is only one area of influence. But if we can give children exposure to as many types of language use as possible, we will better prepare them to be successful in several different settings. When searching for a place in society, children tend to select one that comfortably matches their family's conversation style.

Children are taught to think as they do through continual participation in family conversations. One archaic meaning of "conversation" is "a way of life" (see 2 Corinthians 1:12, Galatians 1:13, Ephesians 2:3). While it is true that people may speak about things they never do, it is also true that our speech reflects our thoughts, which do determine how we act. There is a connection between our way of life and the way we learn to speak. For those of us who want children to live righteously, teaching them the language of the gospel in concept and experience will help prepare them. They will be able to speak of the law written and spoken in their hearts.

11   Faithful Children

It is a wonderful gift for children to believe, to rely on, and to love someone they have not met nor will likely meet in life. Faith in God and in our Redeemer is perhaps the greatest and most fragile of spiritual blessings. It is the basis for a spiritual life. It will be indispensable for the children we hope will rise and bless the next generation.

Faith is a quality of mind, the capacity to believe so strongly that a mental impression is formed of what eyes may not or cannot see and that action results from the belief. Faithfulness in God sustains our efforts and enables us to be constant in our application of gospel principles. When children are truly faithful, they have set themselves on a course of life that will eventually bring them to a full knowledge of all truth.

There are not enough faithful children. Innocent though they begin, they encounter a circumstance of confusion and disillusionment as they grow. One T-shirt I saw announced that the wearer had given up on reality and "was now in search of a good illusion." This might be the announcement of many children who do not seem able to fathom the world and form the light of faith.

Faith is such an important part of our gospel that it surely cannot be a matter of chance that some children are filled with it and others are not. There assuredly must be something we parents can do to increase the likelihood that more of our children will acquire faith, keep it, and use it to build their lives. It is those who are faithful who will be valiant in the testimonies of the Savior. The possibility that parents can help determine whether their children are faithful gives rise to both interest and apprehension. We may be interested in how to teach them but apprehensive about whether we will do it well. Both of these can motivate us to help our children make a place for faithfulness in their minds and hearts.

A Faithful Family

To possess it as individuals, children must first participate in faith with other people. Obviously, families are the earliest, most enduring, and best place for a child to share in becoming a believing person. Families also are excellent examples of the pessimism and cynicism of the unbelieving. Knowing that we can promote either, it is through our interest and devotion that children come to believe in a hopeful way.

There are several ways parents teach the attitude of faithfulness. One occurs, good or bad, because children develop an inner voice made up of what they hear parents say. This inner voice will speak to children when they are about to act. Whether a child will think, "What are my chances of getting caught if . . . " or "what would the Savior do here?" will depend on what he has learned.

The use of inner commands can be first noticed in children just learning to speak. Upon hearing something, children will repeat it as they act it out. Eventually, many actions become so routine that we are unaware of what we say to ourselves, but nevertheless our mind is thinking. This provides us with an opportunity to teach faithfulness. Parents can teach faith, for example, by making positive statements about themselves. This is not arrogance. One kind of statement is a recognition that we do something well–bake bread, wash the car, read books, perform music. In addition, we can make statements that show optimism and hope. Such statements as "Well, it is not an eternal problem," or "This will pass, too," or "Let's keep working and we'll succeed," have helped many to have faith even in adversity. Using these statements or others like them often and over a period of time helps children use them to command their own actions.

Besides what we say about ourselves, children's inner voices repeat what we say to them about themselves. Whether we use critical words or encouraging ones, they become the commands children use to think about themselves. Consider the faith resulting from hearing statements like the following.

A. "It looks hard, but I know you can do it."

B. "By the yard it's hard. By the inch it's a cinch."

C. "I think you can do it."

D. "Sometimes you might want to quit, but I know that you have the ability to finish."

E. "Sure it hurts, but if you will watch closely you can tell the pain goes away."

F. "When you're about to quit, just do one more thing."

G. "I am very proud of you."

H. "You can be whatever you work for."

Encouragement builds faith because it helps children look to a positive future that can be created through their own efforts. While this is taking place without most being aware that faith is growing, children are memorizing the commands they will give to themselves when alone.

In addition, telling children stories, even fantasy stories, can teach faith in specific situations. People and people's experiences are exciting to other people. When we tell about faithful people who prayerfully relied on God, who exemplified enough moral courage to stand true to principle, or who held true to religious beliefs, children are able to understand what faith is in many different settings. Stories have such a profound effect on children that virtually every adult can remember a story told or read to them by a parent. Moreover, most adults have tried to act, at one time or another, like a person they heard about in a story.

Our children first learn about the Savior in stories about Him. We usually tell stories about Jesus thinking that our children should become acquainted with the facts of His life. For this purpose we tell of His birth, events of His ministry, His death and resurrection. We should also recognize that His life is the greatest portrayal of faith we can find. This faith is shown in His belief of God, it is shown by faith in other people, and it is exemplified in a life of exact obedience. We can tell of His love for children, His sadness and loneliness at the disbelief of others, His care for the needy and the sick. We can ask our children what He must have felt when few believed in Him while many rejected Him and sent Him to death. In all this He did not stop believing in us. Even children at a young age can understand that He wants us to believe in and love Him. As they grow older they can also discover that peace and happiness result when we try to be like Him.

Because of their special relationship with children, parents are granted one privilege to promote faith which is given to no other adult. This comes about because parents are the future for their children. If a parent communicates that a child might one day do something special or that certain events should be prepared for, children cannot be indifferent. If the parent-child relationship is positive, children will believe what we explain. If there is conflict they may be skeptical. If there is neglect or hostility, the children will have so little faith in us that they will reject what we tell them.

To promote their ability to be believing, we can form a warm and affectionate relationship and in the midst of it talk about their future possibilities. We do not have to be exact or specific—in fact we might be better not to be. We can say what we think *might* take place or tell about something that *could* happen. Such statements lead children to hope for something good. Such children are those who tackle projects with vigor and announce they will one day present accomplishments to their parents. These children dare to believe in themselves.

One year at Christmastime our family was asked to present the Sunday School program on fast Sunday. We prepared to have the children take turns reading parts of the Christmas story from the scriptures. We took our places on the stand, hopeful that all were prepared. Then during song practice something happened which we had not anticipated. The chorister had invited several people to read a scripture before each song. As it happened, one of the readers read the scriptural verses assigned to one of our sons. As soon as he recognized this he stood up and rushed out of the chapel.

After the program was over I found him sitting in our car embarrassed and determined not to go to class. "Why did she have to do that, Dad?" he asked angrily. I lamely began to explain that she was just trying to do her part. Then, floundering for something more comforting, I impulsively added, "Son, Heavenly Father has sent you here to do an important work." Suddenly all resentment and embarrassment vanished, and my son turned to me and earnestly asked, "What is it, Dad?" I told him about the possibility of a mission, of future church service, and the possibility of leadership. He sat thinking for a moment, then he calmly suggested that we go to our classes.

At first I could not understand what I had done. As I thought about it later I realized that I had simply displaced his unhappiness by giving him hope for something better in the future. He saw some relationship between his future "important work" and the need to go to the Sunday School class.

Parents often motivate their children to practice skills in a similar way. We can inspire young musicians by taking them to a concert or motivate aspiring athletes by taking them to college or professional games. But I have found that this principle can also be used to motivate children to develop faith. When we notice, for example, unique talents in our children, we can encourage them. "Maybe you'll become a writer or a scientist," we might say. If we do this often enough and sincerely enough, our children may have the courage to try out our version of what the future can hold for them because they have learned faith.

Once our children have seen the vision of their future, or believe we believe they have a great future, our parental work is not finished. Often we need to show them how to achieve what they envision and encourage them in their efforts. I have told one of my children who dislikes piano practice that practicing the piano will help him become disciplined enough to be a better athlete, student, missionary, and father. I have also had to get up in the mornings to sit with him as he practiced in order for him to begin achieving his future. As I have tried to apply these ideas in my relationship with my children, I have found a deeper appreciation for Heavenly Father's way of dealing with us. I can understand why obedience to commandments results in the growth of our souls as we develop ourselves for the future time and state of life we call exaltation, and I have begun to find the true joy of parenthood which is found in helping to lead our children toward immortality and eternal life. For parents, this is the significance of Christ's birth and life. He made progression possible and encouraged us to have faith enough to surpass the challenges that development presents to us and to our children.

Finally, faithfulness is taught in our families when we acknowledge God's involvement in our lives. Faith is created when children participate in prayers designed to communicate our hopes and concerns to God. It is instilled when we tell of His answers to our questions. Fasting as a family is a way of deepening our belief and strengthening our devotion to Him. When we choose to avoid carnal conversations, television shows, and movies, children understand that God's spirit is as close as our thoughts. If we want Him to be watchful over us, we must keep our thoughts clean. Private and personal spiritual experiences shared with our children tell them that He is faithful to us and will be to them. We can invite our children to participate in all these foregoing family experiences. Then, throughout childhood and into their adult years, He will always be with them, for they have created a place within for His spirit.

Personal and Public Faith

It will not be enough for us, of course, that our children become only believing people. We will desire that their faithfulness be shown in activities such as missionary service, eternal marriage, and a life of honor and service. Having organized our families to promote the capacity of belief, we then are presented with the task of helping our children demonstrate faith through these important events or works. We usually tell them to "go on missions" or to "marry in the temple" without realizing that children can do both without much faith on their part. Pleasing parents or satisfying a social expectation are all too commonly the reasons felt by many young people for missionary service or temple marriage. Taking time to think this through should easily lead us to understand that this is not what we want. We hope for children to have an inner conviction that such actions are ways of showing their faith in God. Our challenge as parents is to know how to help them get to this point. We are helped in this task by understanding a few things about the way our minds form beliefs and the relationship between personal faith and the faith of people we associate with.

When we understand the physiology of the brain and how it works, it is possible to conclude that our creators prepared in us a foundation for faithfulness. In the same way the human mind learns and thinks about people, it is also able to think of someone who is imaginary. The form of these imaginary people changes as we grow older, but they are always part of our thoughts. Many young children, for example, develop imaginary friends whom they talk to, play with, and think about. Children often talk about them and keep them for several months. Many parents have had to set an extra plate for dinner because a child's "friend" was expected. Sometimes children blame things on their "friend," to their parent's consternation.

This ability to think about the reaction of an imaginary person is an inherited condition, natural to every person. It contributes to the onset of faith, because children are thinking about someone or something as real, though it is not seen. Even children who do not show an elaborate "imaginary friendship" think about the imaginary person. Later, in adolescence, children have an imaginary audience referred to as "they." Parents are told, "they" are all going out for the evening, or "they" are all wearing certain name-brand clothing. This imaginary audience exerts considerable influence even if children cannot specify who "they" really are. The point is that our minds are continuing to share a capacity to believe in and relate to what is not seen.

From the imaginary audience, children "personify" an imagined person, that is, they give this person human traits and characteristics. Those informed about God and His Son usually will "automatically" personify them. God and Christ are then organized in children's minds as individuals with bodies and character traits. This characteristic of human minds, prepared by heavenly parents, is, I believe, the basis of a child's faith in unseen beings.

At the same time that a private faith is emerging, a child has many "public" experiences. If the private, internal experience is not hindered by negative influences and if it matches external experiences—attending church, participating in family prayer, watching people decide to go on missions or marry in the temple—children can develop an authentic faith in God. Their faith increases by being in company with people who give support and exemplify faith to one another. It is because of this that most parents feel a need for a "community of faith" in which to bring their children from infancy to adulthood.

The evidence that children have acquired a deep and everlasting faith in God is found in private acts of loyalty to values and public acts of service and commitment to eternal ideals. The parallel path between children's participation in family and in the "community of faith" (the Church) is shown in table 11.1.

Table 11.1
Parallels in Family and Church Participation

Family	Church
1. Children acquire belief in themselves and are instructed about God and Christ.	1. Children participate in a community of people who teach one another about God and demonstrate faith in the Savior.
2. Children demonstrate ability to imagine individuals who are "real" to them.	2. Stories and accounts of Jesus are applied to children's lives as a group. Children learn that others seem to believe.
3. Children's participation in religious activities at home gives them a chance to demonstrate their personal faith in a private setting.	3. Increased participation in church helps children gain increased confidence as they reflect faithful acts of one another.
4. Personal faith is integrated with the support and encouragement from parents so that children admit to loving their parents and are motivated to turn their private faith into free participation in church activities.	4. Children join the community of faithful by beginning to follow the community's valued behavior. This includes public admission of testimony.
5. The personal faith and public testimony are further integrated as children become focused on desired private acts such as prayer and scripture reading.	5. Children display faith in public ways by rendering mature service, going on missions, and choosing eternal marriage.

Parents who teach their children to be faithful recognize that faith is developed best when families are faithful and children's participation in church is positive. There are many situations when this is not always possible and adaptations need to be made. Some of these situations are listed in table 11.2.

Faith in God and Jesus Christ

The more we know about others and the more we understand or know of them, the more firmly we retain thoughts about them in our minds. This is the reason for the connection between eternal life and knowing the only true God and Jesus Christ whom He sent (John 17:3). Our children's faith in God and in the Savior depends on knowing *about* them. This is the greatness of Joseph Smith's first

Table 11.2
Adapting to Times of Unfaithfulness

Situation	What Parents Can Do
1. Family is faithful, but child has disappointing experiences in church.	A cautious, measured, fact-finding response by parents is enough to show you care but do not side with either the child or representatives of the church. Continuation of positive family experiences is stronger motivation than other isolated experiences. Communicate warmth without taking sides. Inform church personnel in privacy if a change is needed.
2. Famiy life is disrupted and members do not continue regular faithful practices.	Parents will find that only occasionally will people in the church organization compensate for family disruption. While attempting to get extra help for children through the church organization, parents can also (1) evaluate their children's friends for possible support and use them as examples. (2) emphasize that the child has increased personal responsibility for his or her faithful acts. New challenges can be met by increased personal faith, even with less family support. (3) increase the demonstration of their own personal faith and testimony.
3. Some family members become unfaithful and church experiences are not positive.	These are the most difficult situations for faithful experiences. Usually, it is best to increase exposure of children to others who exhibit desired faithful behavior (e.g., missionaries' experiences, young people enthused about the gospel). Learn what appeals to children and use it to impel them to participate (sports, dance, drama, etc.). Patience and calm perseverance usually succeed when accompanied by declarations of personal faith.
4. Some family members are not faithful, but church experiences are positive.	Use discrepancy between church experiences and the values of other family members to teach acceptance and support for those of a different faith. Contrast often helps children strengthen personal and public faithfulness. Attempt, therefore, to avoid choosing sides.

vision. From it we learn about the identity of these two eternal personages as divine men. We also learn they have an intimate knowledge of Joseph Smith. God's statement, "[Joseph], This is My Beloved Son," lets us appreciate they have an intimate awareness of all human beings.

Faith in the Savior and in God is often a belief based on knowledge *about* them. Faith may start out as a testimony that they live, that Christ is the Redeemer. But for the spiritually mature, this faith becomes a full relationship of love for them and a life of commitment to honor them by obedience. Our children usually deepen and expand their faith according to how much they know. The more they know *about* God and the Savior, the more likely they are to firmly believe in them.

The relationship between the spiritually mature person and his God comes from experiences which enable that person to know *of* Him. We can learn about Him through scriptural knowledge and words of the prophets, but knowing *of* Him only takes place by doing what He has done. I learned some of the truth of this idea one winter day when I was walking toward campus. I was an undergraduate student living in the men's dormitories at Brigham Young University. My path to the campus was up a wide cement ramp bordered by shrubs and flowers. The lower half of the ramp covered a major pipe from the heating plant, and as a result any snow that fell soon melted. The upper half and steepest part, however, could be very slippery.

There was a student in the dorms that year who had suffered a childhood disease that left him spastic. His unimpaired intellect allowed him to converse with people and to be successful in school work. It was customary to see him make his way around campus in a shuffling, awkward gait, or occasionally riding in a motorized chair. On this overcast wintery day, he was walking toward campus up the ramp a few feet ahead of me. It began to snow. The lower part of the ramp was all right, but snow had collected on the upper part, and it was quite slippery. He slowed down as he climbed, and many who passed asked if they could help. He declined and slowed his pace even more. I passed him just as he reached the level sidewalk at the top and prepared to cross the intersection. We stepped off the curb together, and as his feet came down he slipped and suddenly fell to the ground. Textbooks, notebooks, and pencils flew in the air. As if with one mind, every student who witnessed this stopped, each to help. I was close, so I picked up a book and a pen. Two boys picked him up. A girl gathered up a notebook and stood brushing the snow from it.

Through his embarrassment, he tried to say thanks and appeared to just want to get on his way. In a brief, brilliant moment, we all looked into each others' eyes and without saying a word turned to our destinations. A lump filled my throat, and I heard Christ's disciples of old asking, "Master, who did sin, this man, or his parents? . . . Jesus answered, Neither hath this man sinned, nor his parents: but that the works of God should be made manifest in him." (John 9:2-3.) I looked up and saw that the girl with the notebook was watching me. She smiled, and I smiled back. The two boys were nearby, and I looked for them. They were looking intently at us. I nodded to them and they to me, the eloquence of the moment unbroken by words. We each felt it and knew the others did, too. At that moment I knew more of the Savior, for I knew I had felt what He felt.

Missionaries know *of* Him because their work is so much like His. Compassionate people know *of* Him through their loving care. Givers to the poor, the humble and the meek, those who fast and are prayerful, know of Him. Those who sacrifice for others and love as He loved know of Him. Those who obey and know of His doctrine also know of Him. We know because the spirit within resonates when we learn more. Faithful children who form a relationship with the Savior and our Eternal Father are those who have acted as They have acted. Then, our children have faith in Jesus Christ and know that He knows of it. A lifetime of loving and faithful service will be given in His name. These children are those who offer the ancient sacrifice made eternal through the redemption of Christ. They will write His name upon their countenances and give to Him humble and contrite hearts.

12   Children's Spirits

Because our children develop gradually, we can always have hope for their future. As we watch them get better at whatever they try, we feel satisfaction in their achievements and confidence that they will continue to succeed in what they want to do. As they gradually become adults we enjoy sharing the experience with them; we feel in their maturing. It is as if we have known what they would be like, and to see them finally filling the spaces of our dreams is a wonderful thing.

Without much calculation on our part, our watching, measuring, teaching, and sharing have led us to form ideas about what they might become. Since as children they have not yet reached what we dream for them, part of their relationship with us is a mental or spiritual impression we have for each child. Then, as they grow and better find and become themselves, it is a great delight to see them match or improve on our expectations. Sometimes, for a while, our children do not grow toward this ideal. It is a terrible mistake for us to forget that they are not finished and to begin to tell them how badly they are doing. All forms of parental abuse are the words and actions of people who have forgotten this great truth. In forgetting, we say things or treat children in ways that mean we think our children are failing and there is no future left in which to improve.

The harshness and hurt some parents inflict on their children may bruise their bodies, but most often the greatest wounds are those done to their spirits. When my three oldest children were small, they entered our living room one day quiet, white-faced, and subdued. "Why aren't you playing?" I asked. "I don't feel like it," the oldest replied. The other two nodded agreement, and so I asked,

"What is the matter?" My daughter began to cry and told through her tears that they had witnessed a terrible fight between a father and son. The father had hit the boy on the back with a shovel. Though many years have passed, I think my children have not forgotten witnessing this event.

I am sure that the father would like to take that day back and redo it. The flash of unrestrained anger probably is an embarrassment to him now. Nevertheless, that event and others like it leave indelible marks on children. We can know, profoundly know, of the good that love does by understanding the effects of its absence. Children's spirits sag if the weight of this life is heavy and must be borne with intense soberness. It takes the light from their eyes, the joy from their childhood.

When we are able to love them, play with them, touch them, laugh with and at them, and carefully nurture them as they grow, children thrive, blossoming in the warmth of it all. What they actually do and become is closer then to our best dreams for them. We will have loved and cherished them to a true and hopeful life. When asked the reason for his successful children, one father said, "My wife and I thank the Lord in family prayer for the great children He has given to us." They transfer this gratitude to the understanding of their children by their attitudes and actions. Then, believing they are loved and being nurtured by caring parents, the children can make a place in their minds and hearts for the whisperings of a spirit voice that brings all truth to them.

These are children who have a sense of sacred things, who recognize our Father's voice, and who rely on it to live. These children yearn to have the companionship of that Spirit who brings peace of mind. In what they see in life, they can discern between that which is worldly and of short-term worth and that which is spiritually enduring. They are spiritually born of God.

The Point of Reference

The sound of God's spirit is usually felt and understood inside us. When we speak of listening to this voice, we really mean that we are reflecting or meditating. This requires us to focus our attention in and away from what is external to us.

Young children are more tuned to other people, to objects, and to touch and taste than they are to their own thoughts. If we nurture and protect it, there is a natural gradual shift to more self-awareness as they grow. But if something or someone frightens, hurts, or confuses them, they will be more likely to learn to keep the focus of attention away from themselves. This is done, of course, in order to hide and protect their feelings. Love, in contrast, makes children feel safe about their environment and allows them to think about themselves. Over time, this self-reflection enables them to develop an ability to be secure about their thoughts and feelings instead of being overly concerned about the opinions of others.

There are other things parents can do to help children reflect on themselves. One of these is to express empathy. Empathy is acknowledging that one person recognizes another's emotions and also to some degree senses what is felt by the other. Empathy between parents and children confirms children's own emotions and improves their capacity for empathy with others. Children appear to be born with some ability for empathy, because even an infant will respond to another infant's distress, and by the age of three or four a child can find reasonable solutions to the needs of another. Therefore, if children do not develop a mature empathy for others, it is usually because they spend time with people who do not nurture it.

Empathy requires that we look past the obvious aspects of a child's actions and search for an underlying emotion. Then our voice tones, words, and other actions must be appropriate for their feelings. These conditions convince children that their way of thinking about things is all right, even if we must correct them later.

I happened onto the importance of empathy by chance late one night. My three-and-a-half-year-old son had awakened and told me there were snakes in his bed. I could have simply told him to go back to bed, since I was tired. But I got up and, with his hand in mine, walked to his bed. I found striped sheets and knew where the idea of snakes had originated. I could and usually would have explained this to the child, trying to improve his understanding. Instead, I grabbed a book and vigorously slammed it on the bed several times. Then I turned and said, "I got them, son." He matter-of-factly replied, "Thanks, Dad," and then climbed into bed. Without thinking about it, I had correctly guessed his need for assurance, responded in a way that looked appropriate to him, and communicated to him that his thoughts were not ludicrous.

Besides helping them notice their own natural empathy, parents can help children focus on their own thoughts and feelings by asking about them. Some research about parent-child communication yielded results that suggest many parents tell and interrogate more than they ask about children's thoughts and try to understand them. Such conversational skills can be learned with a little practice. They direct children's attention to their own opinons and feelings.

We can also help children focus on themselves by asking them to assess how they acted in many situations. Most people accurately recall less than 30 percent of what they do during a particular episode in their lives. That is because they are watching or reacting to something or someone else. We can encourage our children to evaluate themselves by asking, "What did you do?" then "What happened next?" and so on until children have described their actions in a sequence with what others did. If this is done often, children will begin to think about themselves while they are acting. This, along with empathy and questioning to understand, will help children give enough attention to what they sense within to help prepare them for the most important spiritual training.

Reverence, Prayer, and Repentance

We hold sacred our God, His Son, the Holy Ghost, and any place or scripture that symbolizes them. Reverence is the worshipping of these beings by treating their names, times, places, and ceremonies dedicated to them as holy. This means that we display special attitudes and actions when we focus on these things. That is why we are to change our ordinary routine on the Sabbath day. This is one way we honor the Son of God.

The attitude and actions of reverence appropriate for sacred occasions are often difficult for children to learn. The actions are usually quiet thoughtfulness and the absence of unruly behavior. The attitudes of reverence include gratitude, love, and remembering the greatness of the divine people and what they do for us. Usually children can perform the actions before they learn the attitude. In the process, parents realize the frustrations associated with teaching that something is to be done at one time that is not always required of them. Some spank their children, some get angry, and others let their children do whatever they usually do. The most effective tool is practice. If children do not show the actions of reverence in one place, take them to another room and require they do it there until they are ready to return. If they learn there is no escape, they will usually learn quickly.

Reverent actions of a child are first taught by example, then by a cue to begin, and then emulated because others are praised. Eventually, these actions are associated with the attitude of reverence toward God and His Son. When we help our children act reverently as they are thinking about Heavenly Father and the Savior, eventually actions and attitudes are inseparably connected. Thereafter, a place, a time, or sacred names will remind them, and they will feel a spiritual closeness to sacred beings.

As our children grow and repeat reverent actions in the special times and places that require reverence, they will improve their spiritual communication. Reverence prepares the soul to receive the testimony of the Holy Ghost about God and His Son. This testimony is borne, as we know, to the spirit of each person. Children's capacity for spiritual communication gradually increases, and they come to yearn for companionship of the Holy Ghost. Then children will live righteously in order to have it. When someone chooses to do or not do something in order to preserve the spiritual light, he or she is spiritually mature.

One special reverent act is that of prayer. We think of it as communication between man and God, which assuredly it is. But it is in its truest sense also a display of reverence toward God. As the Savior instructed, if prayer is too ritualized, it is a vain display and not of the heart.

When we teach children to pray, we often give them simple lines which they repeat at prayer times. Too often, as they grow, the words change but still are spoken in the simple lines of the young. Instead, reverent prayer takes place when children tell their thoughts and feelings to God. The more they share, the more they will receive in return. We can teach children to pray by first having a conversation with them which helps them think about their daily experiences. When they tell us how they have acted, thought, or felt, we can invite them to also tell Heavenly Father. When children pray in this fashion, it is easier for them to also identify their specific needs. Instead of a general "blessing" ("bless the leaders of the Church"), children will know what they should say and why.

Because prayers of the heart are truly answered, our children will receive more answers to their prayers and more surely know God loves and is close to them. A prayer relationship will begin that draws our children closer to God, becomes more tender, and sustains our children throughout their lives.

Among the several things we can do to show reverence for Jesus Christ, there is one thing other than prayer, that best acknowledges His atoning sacrifice. This is the act and attitude of repentance. Having been taught that faith in the Lord Jesus Christ is a necessary condition for spiritual growth, it remains that repentance is the most relevant ceremony to acknowledge that we accept Him as our Savior. All who sincerely repent will know that He does wash the guilt away through a forgiving love.

To help our children understand spiritual things, we can teach them the actions and attitudes of repentance as a way to show reverence for the Savior. A young child brought some modeling clay home from school that his parents knew did not belong to him. At first the child denied any wrongdoing, but through the calm and loving conversation with his father, he admitted what he had done. He was thanked for telling the truth, then he was asked what should be done. "I'll just take it back," he said. "Taking it back is a good idea," his father replied, "but it doesn't seem like that is enough." The boy sat in silence, not knowing what else to say. "I wonder," his dad continued, "if you shouldn't tell the teacher what has happened and say you are sorry." His face whitened a little, and the boy shook his head, "No." "I will write a note and tell your teacher you have something to say to her." "I won't do it!" the boy stated. "Why do I have to?" "Because," his father explained, "you have taken something she is responsible for. You can tell her you are sorry for what you have done and then feel happier after you have done it. If you just take it back, you might still feel unhappy." The boy got up and left the room. Both went to bed. In the morning the father prepared the note, encouraged the boy who finally promised to give it to the teacher, and they left for school and work. Later in the day this father called the boy and asked him what he had done. After hearing his son had completed the task, the father was silent for a moment. "I am proud of you," he said. "You have shown real courage."

While he is young the boy will know only that he has to stop taking clay from school. As he grows and learns about the Atonement, he will recognize that he used the Savior's method to correct what is done wrong. If there is a need to repent of other things, he will learn spiritually that Christ is his Redeemer. Repentance shows reverence for the Savior's great sacrifice. While parents hope that repentance is seldom necessary, teaching our children this sacred ceremony of forgiveness will help them love the Savior for His great gift to them.

Our Children's Vision

The writer of Proverbs wrote, "Where there is no vision, the people perish" (Proverbs 29:18). Scriptural scholars usually interpret this to mean that revelation is necessary for a people to continue in righteousness. There is another interpretation of this scripture that relates to our children. If we conclude that a vision is a spiritual gift to anyone who lives righteously and that it is a guiding sense or impression of what is to come, then without an idea or vision of their future, children are more aimless, more vulnerable to temptation, and in greater risk of perishing. This vision and the discernment that accompanies it are spiritual gifts that may be granted to those who are blessed by them.

When we teach our children to recognize and appreciate spiritual things and to live accordingly, a natural outgrowth is a sense of personal vision. This is not a visitation of angels or the sight of intense light; it is an impression of what might be, what can be, and if worked at, what will be. It is as subtle as the quick glimpse of a single thought. Children may at first "see" themselves in sports, being popular with friends, wearing new clothes, or winning awards. As those visions are practiced, spiritual whisperings begin to help children "see" themselves on missions, teaching Sunday School, in temples, and caring for the welfare of others.

There is abundant spiritual and earthly evidence that these thoughts of the future exert great influence on what people do. As we prepare our children to seek the guidance of the Lord's spirit, we are also helping implant a vision within their minds. These impressions, stimulated by the example of others, fireside talks, conversations with friends, and encouragement from parents will lead children in correct paths. Children will pursue activities which lead to the realization of these small but significant views of the future.

It is not a large step from this for children to extend their vision of earthly achievements to those of a heavenly nature. Looking forward to living with God, to being with a family eternally, and to finding exaltation are visions of what may be. When these exist in the thoughts of our children, they will move and grow toward them as well. The laws of the gospel will be understood by them as the necessary preparation for achieving what they envision. They will try and succeed, stumble occasionally, and try again. The visions of what is possible will help them rise from discouragement, give them hope, and keep them going. Their hearts will not fail them in our latter days, because they have filled their hearts with the nourishment of God's law. They can stand nobly and confidently because the derision, temptation, and ridicule of others is less important than achieving the vision granted them. We, this generation of parents in Israel, will have accomplished our vision. Our children will be prepared to carry on our covenant, our gospel, and our lineage. We and they will have eternal lives.

Index

Father, of newborn, 27
Fathers, birth witnessed by, 25
Family, faith taught in , 132–33
    influence of, on children, 120
    violent crime in, 19
Family environment, 121–23
    learning in, 123–25
Family pilgrimage, 11–12
Father's blessing, 120
Foreordination, 119
Forgiveness, 53
Freedom, in a good relationship, 48
    through choices, 71
Friends, 22
Future, children look to, 81, 135
    personal vision of, 148–49

God, children taught by, 3
    children taught to know, 8–9
    value of human life to, 19–20
Godhood, potiential of each child for, 6
Golden, Constance, 5
Gospel, child development aided by, 4
    children to be taught, 8, 19
    children develop understanding of, 3
    inner understanding of, 2
    love taught by, 21
    Savior's introduction of, 40–41
"Growth potential," 6,8

Heavenly Father. *See* God
Higgs, Jesse, 13
Homework, and son who procrastinated,
    70–71
Honesty, 99–102
    teaching children about, 102–4
Human life, valued by Savior, 19
Human progression, 17
    See also Progression
Humans, of divine parentage, 19
Hymes, James, 56

Ideas, selection of, 15
Identical twins, story about, 5–6
Identity, development of, 6
    importance of child's, 96–97
    importance of personal, 95–96
    transmitted from parent to child, 97–98
Imaginary friends, 136–37
Immaturity, behavior due to, 2
Inherited traits, 5–6
Inner qualities, 21
Insecure attachments, 26
Israelites, 39–40

Jefferson, Charles, 83
Jeremiah, 8
Jesus Christ. *See* Savior

Language, environment shaped by, 30, 31
    function of, 128–29
    table illustrating seven uses of, 130
Law of Moses, 40–41
Little league baseball game, story about,
    33–34
Love, communication of, 22–23
    developing through, 21
    forgiveness achieved by, 53–54
    importance of knowing, 25
    in a good relationship, 48
    of children, 19–20
Lucifer, 10

Marriage, 25
McConkie, Bruce R., 53
Meditation, 143–44
Mental needs, 22
Misbehavior, attention through, 2
    change of, 55, 61
    illustrative table, 57, 64
    of children, 20
    understanding of, 55–56
Missionaries, at MTC, 1
    author's family contacted by, 12
Missionary, at MTC, 9–10
Moses, 94

Nephite children, 19
New neighborhood, move to, 22–23

Obedience, 39

Parenthood, comprehension of, 15
    in eternal progression, 18
    increasing pleasure of, 17–18
    observation a part of, 4
Parenting, child-centered, 16
    overly concerned, 16
Parents, adaptation to children, 7
    relationship between children and, 4,
        20–23, 90
    table illustrating effect of achievers on,
        91
    worth of children to, 20
Personal vision, 148–49
Personality, 4
Personality traits, inheritance of, 5–6
Peter the Apostle, 61